THE
FIVE LEVELS
OF
ATTACHMENT

THE
FIVE LEVELS
OF
ATTACHMENT

DON MIGUEL
RUIZ JR.

Hierophant publishing

Cover design by Emma Smith
Cover art © Lukiyanova Natalia / frenta / Shutterstock
Text design by Jane Hagaman

Hierophant Publishing
8301 Broadway, Suite 219
San Antonio, TX 78209
888-800-4240
www.hierophantpublishing.com

If you are unable to order this book from your local
bookseller, you may order directly from the publisher.

Library of Congress Control Number: 2012954093

ISBN 978-1-938289-45-3

10 9 8 7

Dedication

To all whom I love

Among individuals, as among nations,
respect for the rights of others is peace.

—Benito Juarez

Contents

Foreword

Don Miguel Ruiz Jr., my first son, belongs to a new gen-
eration of artists, Toltecs, who are transforming the way of
life of our beloved humanity.

My son has spent a great portion of his life silently
rebelling against the way other people live, creating many
judgments and opinions. He did not realize that in doing
so, he was becoming attached to those judgments and
opinions, and his emotional reactions were becoming
increasingly intense.

One day he had a conversation with his grandmother—
a conversation that would forever change his life. During
this conversation, his grandmother, a faith healer, helped
him understand the attachment she had to the rituals she
used for healing her patients. My son saw his own reflection in this interaction with his grandmother and was able

to clearly see all of his attachments. This is how his rebellion came to an end.

Although it took him a couple of years to completely assimilate this experience into his life, he finally decided to share it in a book. *The Five Levels of Attachment* is that book, and it is destined to transform the lives of millions of readers. It is written in a way that is simple, congruent, and easy to understand.

This book will help you gain awareness of how your attachments have created your reality, and how your belief system has been making all the decisions in the story of your life. It will also help you see how you create your identity based on the opinions and judgments of others around you. Don Miguel Ruiz Jr. explains how our beliefs become intimately connected to our identity, or who we think we are. This belief of what the truth is in turn creates all our attachments and all our emotional responses.

He also explains how our attachment to our beliefs distorts our perceptions, allowing us to readjust our perceptions until they conform to the rest of our belief system. This awareness helps us to easily understand how we create our own superstitions and might become fanatics of our own attachments.

He helps us realize that although we live in the present, our attachment makes us dream of a past that no longer exists, a past that is full of regret and drama. Our attachments also take us to an uncertain future full of fears that do not yet exist, making us feel unsafe.

By explaining how our attachments can be divided into five levels of intensity, he teaches us how to assess our own attachment to any particular belief that we have, and points out that the majority of the world's population lives within levels three and four, Identity and Internalization.

As you will see, don Miguel Jr. clearly states the influence attachment has over the decisions we make when designing the story of our life, and how these attachments move us away from reality. He also offers very effective tools that will help us improve the way we handle our levels of attachment and our resulting emotional reactions. This improvement will be reflected in the interactions we have with those around us, especially our loved ones.

This book is definitely destined to become a classic—one you will surely be reading again and again.

—DON MIGUEL RUIZ

Introduction

Everything is made of light. We are the stars;
and the stars are us. When we see this, all
of our senses are truly open and there is no
need to interpret the world. In this moment,
our full, unlimited potential is available to
us. There is nothing blocking our way. . . .

—DON MIGUEL RUIZ, *THE FOUR AGREEMENTS*

My father, don Miguel Ruiz, a teacher and retired medical doctor, spent many thoughtful and transformative years interpreting our Toltec traditions to fit the world we live in today. The Toltecs were great women and men of knowledge who lived thousands of years ago in the area that is now known as south central Mexico. In the

Nahuatl language, *Toltec* means "artist," and according to our teachings, the canvas for our art is life itself. I learned about the Toltec way of life through the oral traditions of my family, who (according to my paternal great-great-grandfather, don Exiquio) are direct descendants of the Toltecs of the Eagle Knight lineage. This knowledge came to me by way of my grandmother, Madre Sarita.

We call ourselves Toltecs not just because of our lineage, but because we are artists. Life is the canvas of our art, and the work of our tradition is to teach the life lessons that will help us create our masterpiece.

The Toltec tradition is not a religion, but rather a way of life in which our great masterpiece is living in happiness and love. It embraces spirit while honoring the great many masters of all of the world's traditions. The whole point of all this work is to be happy, to enjoy life, and to enjoy the relationships with the people we love the most, starting with oneself.

I began my apprenticeship into my family's tradition in San Diego, California, when I was fourteen years old. My seventy-nine-year-old grandmother, Madre Sarita, was my teacher and the spiritual head of our family. She was a *curandera,* a faith healer who helped people in her small temple in Barrio Logan, a neighborhood in San Diego, with the power of her faith in God and love. Since my father was a medical doctor, the juxtaposition of the two forms of healing allowed me to see our tradition through different points of view.

I appreciated the power of my grandmother's words long before I had a firm grasp of their meaning. I also saw things that others could only describe as "magic" transformed into everyday happenings; miraculous healings were the norm for Madre Sarita. I still felt a strong pull from the outside world, though—the allure of hanging out with my friends, of being like everyone else. I moved back and forth between the Toltec world of my family and the mainstream world of school and friends, constantly struggling to find a way to combine my experiences and yet keep them separate at the same time.

Though she spoke no English, my grandmother gave sermons and lectures across the country. My apprenticeship began with translating my grandmother's lectures from Spanish to English. For many years, I awkwardly stumbled over her words, and my grandmother would just look at me and laugh.

One day she asked me if I knew why I stumbled. I had all sorts of answers: you are speaking too quickly, you don't give me a chance to catch up, some words don't have a direct translation. . . . She just looked at me silently for a few moments and then asked, "Are you using knowledge, or is knowledge using you?"

I looked at her blankly. She continued, "When you translate, you try to express my words through what you already know, what you think is true. You do not hear me; you hear yourself. Imagine doing the same thing every single moment in life. If you are looking through life and translating it as it goes along, you will miss out on living it. But if you learn to *listen* to life, you will always be able to express the words as they come. Your knowledge has to become a tool you will use to guide you through life but that can also be put aside. Do not let knowledge translate everything you experience."

I nodded in response, but it didn't dawn on me until many years later what my grandmother was truly talking about. Throughout life, we constantly narrate, or commentate on, everything we do, say, see, touch, smell, taste, and hear. As natural storytellers, we continuously keep the plot moving forward, sometimes missing millions of subplots that are developing on their own. It is like taking a sip of wine and saying, "It's a bit dry; it has definitely aged well, but I can taste the bark. I've had better." Instead of simply experiencing the joy and flavors of the wine, we are analyzing the flavor, trying to break it down and fit it into a context and language we already know. In doing this, we miss out on much of the actual experience.

This is a simple example of how we narrate life—explaining it, but, more importantly, justifying and judging it. Instead of taking an experience for what it is, we create a story to make it fit our beliefs. During Madre Sarita's talks, I had to completely shut down my thoughts, because if my mind's commentary got in the way I would miss out on her message. With this simple process, my grandmother showed me that if we only see the world through the filters of our preconceptions, we are going to miss out on actually living. After much practice, I eventually learned to close my eyes, shut out the world that existed outside my head and the voice of knowledge inside my head, and translate *every single word* she said accurately.

Seeing beyond our filters—our accumulated knowledge and beliefs—does not always come naturally. We have spent years growing attached to them in various degrees, and they feel safe. Whatever we become attached to can begin to shape our future experiences and limit our perception of what exists outside our vocabulary. Like blinders on a horse, our attached beliefs limit our vision, and this in turn limits our perceived direction in life. The stronger our level of attachment, the less we can see.

Think about your set of attached beliefs as a unique melody repeating itself in your mind. In a way, we are constantly trying to force our melody—the one we have become accustomed to hearing—onto other melodies, without realizing that often the melody is not our own, and perhaps it's not even the one we want to be playing. If we continue playing only what we know, never opening ourselves to listen to the other songs flowing around us, we are letting our attachment to our particular melody control us. Instead, choose to listen to other melodies playing. Perhaps you will contribute to them, adding a harmony or a bass line and just seeing where the music takes you. By letting go of your attachment to what you think the melody *should* be, you open yourself to the potential to create a unique and beautiful song of your own composition or a collaboration that can be shared with others.

In this book, I will teach you the Five Levels of Attachment. They are guideposts for gauging how attached you are to your own point of view, as well as how open you are to other opinions and possibilities. As the level of attachment increases, one's identity, the "who I am," becomes more directly linked with knowledge, or the "what I know."

Knowledge and the information we perceive are distorted and corrupted by our narrators—the voices of our thoughts that debate the rightness or wrongness of every action we take and every thought we have. When we believe in something so strongly that we lose the awareness of our Authentic Self within the stories and comments of our internal narrators, we are allowing our preconceptions to make our decisions for us. Therefore, it is important to be aware of where we are on the scale of attachment with any particular belief. With awareness, we can regain the power to make our own decisions.

It is my hope that you will engage this book to measure how attached you are to various beliefs and ideas in your life that create your reality, your Personal Dream, and contribute to our collective reality and the Dream of the Planet. Only with this deeper awareness of yourself are you truly free to pursue your passion and experience your full potential. The choice is up to you!

CHAPTER I

An Exploration of Perception and Potential

Our point of view creates our reality. When we are stuck in our beliefs, our reality becomes rigid, stagnant, and oppressive. We become bound to our attachments because we have lost our ability to recognize that we have a choice to be free of them.

When we look at ourselves in the mirror, we often hear a narrative in our mind of what we see, a definition of self in the form of an identity that is based on our "agreements"—the thoughts and beliefs we have said yes to. This identity stems from ideological beliefs that have come to us over a period of time from our family, culture, religion, education, friends, and beyond, and these beliefs are encapsulated into a single system that is represented in the reflected image of a physical living being—in my case, a living being named Miguel Ruiz Jr., with a point of view that is uniquely my own.

Each one of my agreements represents an attachment I have created for myself over the course of my lifetime. For example, when I look into the mirror, I perceive myself in this way:

I am . . .

- Miguel

- a Toltec

- a *nagual* (a spiritual guide)

- a Mexican-American

- an American

- a mestizo

- a husband

- a father

- a writer

and so on . . .

This list of self-definitions is my reflection, and when I really look at myself, I can hear the narration of my agreements and the conditions that have become my model for self-acceptance. My thoughts are the narrators of my attachments, my belief system.

I project onto the image of myself the values and attributes that reflect my beliefs. The more attached I am to my beliefs, the more difficult it becomes to see myself for who I am at this moment, and the less freedom I have to see life from a fresh perspective and perhaps choose a different path. As my attachments become more intense and more entrenched, I lose the awareness of my Authentic Self as it becomes obscured by the filters of my belief system. In the Toltec tradition, we call this the *Smokey Mirror*—the smoke that doesn't allow us to perceive our Authentic Self.

What gives these attachments their strength is *conditional* love. When you look in the mirror, instead of accepting yourself for who you are at this very moment, you likely start telling yourself why you are unacceptable in your current form, and what you need to do to be able to accept yourself: *I must meet this expectation to be worthy of my own love.*

The desire to obtain the flawless fulfillment of the archetypal model of each one of my agreements distorts my reflection even more. I begin to judge and evaluate myself according to the standards of my agreements, which have turned into the conditions for self-acceptance. I implement a system of reward and punishment to train myself to reach that archetypal model; this is known in the Toltec tradition as *domestication*.

The primary tool used to domesticate oneself is self-judgment. Using my archetypal model of what "I am Miguel" is supposed to mean, I see upon looking at my reflection all the perceived flaws or inadequacies, and my domestication springs into action:

- "I'm not smart enough."
- "I'm not attractive enough."
- "I don't have enough."
- "I'm lacking this or that."

and so on.

Self-judgment resides where self-acceptance wishes to be. Our attachment to these negative beliefs and self-judgments can become so normal that we don't even recognize them as condemnations anymore; we accept them as a part of who we are. But at a very basic level, our self-judgments are all consequences of what we believe about ourselves at our core—whether we accept or reject ourselves.

Of all the beliefs to detach from, this is the most important one: *Let go of the attachment that you must obtain some image of perfection in order to be happy.* And this isn't only about appearances; it includes the way we think, the philosophy we follow, our spiritual pursuits, and our place in society. All these things are conditions upon which we accept ourselves. We think that in order to be worthy of our own love we must live up to the expectations we place on ourselves—but we need to realize that these expectations are the expression of our agreements, not of our true nature.

Ironically, it is often at the moment that we have the opportunity to see our truth—when we are faced with our reflection, whether in a mirror or outside in the world— that the narrators speak the loudest. I know of people, myself included, who have refused to look at themselves in the mirror because the self-judgments were deafening. It is impossible for people—teens and adults alike—to live up to an illusion.

Of course, it's easy to blame our media, our culture, or our community for perpetuating images of what is expected of us. We are flooded with commercials and archetypal images of heroes and heroines, beautiful damsels in distress and professional athletes, examples of ugliness and how *not* to be. But at the very core of it, there is no one to blame, because a commercial, like self-judgment, has no power over us unless we agree with its message. It is only when we willingly attach ourselves to these images and distortions that our happiness is compromised.

We do not need to take the blame for these self-judgments. We can simply become aware that they have been developing in our lives since childhood through the process of domestication. Once we are aware of our self-judgments, we can reclaim our freedom by choosing for ourselves to transcend the rewards and punishment model that has been imposed upon us to eventually arrive at a place of self-acceptance.

We have a choice. . . . That is our power.

When you look into the mirror, you are the only one who can hear your narrators; only you know what those self-judgments are. They take whatever voice and shape you give them, but they are only the expression of something you've already said yes to. You can make the choice to detach yourself from the standards that create an unrealistic image of yourself by knowing that you have the power to say no. When you no longer believe in a self-judgment, it will no longer have any power over you. You can choose to view yourself from a place of acceptance based on the undeniable truth that you are already perfect and complete exactly the way you are right now.

From this point of view, you may still choose to make some life changes; but now the motivation to change is not because you hope to someday love yourself but because you *already do* love yourself. When the reflection is viewed from this angle, change flows in synchronicity with the trajectory of your life, and the possibilities are limitless. Suffering only occurs when we forget that.

Mistaking Perfection for Imperfection

When my father first tried to get me to understand that I am perfect, I found it impossible to accept. I tried to understand, but I couldn't. I was attached to my belief that perfection is something to be attained through hard work and dedication—and I still had a long way to go. How could I be perfect? I hadn't yet accomplished my goals: I wasn't what I wanted to be. I couldn't attract the girl I wanted. I didn't weigh what I thought I should weigh. On and on I went with my diatribe, managing to ascertain and then judge all of my imperfections.

With this kind of perfection, whenever our story does

not match our beliefs, we judge it as imperfect; then we punish ourselves for not living up to our beliefs of how we think we should live. We eventually acquire a definition of perfection that has nothing to do with actual perfection: "being free from all flaws or defects." Most often, we read this definition through the eyes of judgment, from the point of view of someone outside who's trying to live up to the stories we've created about ourselves.

If we do happen to achieve perfection momentarily from this point of view, we reward ourselves with conditional self-love. Then we use conditional self-love as our motivator to pursue this distorted idea of perfection in the future. It's a circuitous problem.

I continued to struggle with this concept as I grew older. Still, my father persisted throughout the years with this message. He told me, "Miguel, when you understand that you are perfect just the way you are, you will see that everything is perfect just the way it is."

It's not easy to just wake up one day and say you're perfect and actually believe it. It requires desire and commitment. First, you leave behind any false ideals of perfection—you release your attachment to what you believe it means to be the perfect you. In order to learn this lesson, I needed to stop judging myself for not meeting my own expectations and accept myself for who I am at this very moment. I began at the beginning, learning to love myself and giving gratitude every morning for being alive.

Second, you view life through the eyes of an artist and accept that everything is a work in progress, a never-ending masterpiece. Every brushstroke is perfect simply because it exists. As the paint hits the canvas, it grows and develops into what it is—even if we don't always have an outline to keep us in the lines. Whether colorful scribbles or a detailed landscape, each element of the piece is fulfilling and complete, even as we continue to paint, changing and evolving with every stroke of life. As my father says, "Our life is a canvas, and we are all Picassos."

From an early age, it is engrained in almost every one of us that we must achieve certain ideals or become "somebody" in order to be worthy of our own acceptance, of our own love. Existing within this as-soon-as-I-have-this or once-I-do-that mentality chains us to the belief that we are not free to live our lives now.

Many of us are familiar with Miguel de Cervantes' great literary masterpiece *Don Quixote*. In it, retired gentleman Alonso Quijano moves to La Mancha and becomes so caught up in books of chivalry that his sense of reality becomes so distorted his identity transforms into the character of don Quixote. He sees the world through filters of fantasy and adventure. Whatever reality presents, don Quixote redirects the story to fit his own expectations and beliefs. By the end, our hero is defeated and dejected, chasing after an image that forever eludes him.

Like don Quixote, we are constantly investing ourselves into the stories we want to believe. We create our own personas so that we are "somebody." When I was young, I took on various identities. I was Miguel Ruiz Jr., the Goth. Then I became Miguel the Intellectual, then Miguel the Bohemian, then Miguel the Artist, and so on. I gave myself rules the same way don Quixote created his rules—through a distorted perception of who I was. Other people would see their own truth and wonder what I was doing. But all I saw was what I wanted to see. And like don Quixote's faithful servant Sancho Panza, I heard my stories and knew I was being a little crazy, but I believed them just in case I was right.

I spent many years trying to live up to those images I created of myself before discovering that *this* is who I am—no story needed. It's really me. I am perfect at this very moment, and that is all I need to enjoy my life. Once I learned this, I could change my life in any direction

I saw fit at any given moment. I now had the freedom to choose. The possibilities became endless, just as they always had been. I do not make changes in my life today because I feel I must change in order to accept and love myself; I make changes to express myself and experience more of life, because I already accept and love myself for who I am.

Flaws and defects originate from our own ideas and beliefs. In order to recognize perfection—or to see the world and ourselves *as is*—we become aware of our attachments to our ideas and beliefs and let go of them, even if only briefly, to see beyond them. I have always been perfect, and so have you. When we can't perceive this, it's because we are too busy judging everything for not being something other than what it is. The world and everything in it is perfect simply because it exists at this very moment, in the only manner it can possibly exist. The same is true for me and for you. And that is perfection: "I am because I am at this moment."

This is what freedom is: the ability to enjoy and be exactly who you are without suppressing yourself in the form of judgment. A bird is a bird. A saguaro is a saguaro. A human is a human. Miguel is Miguel. You are you. Perfect.

From that point of view, change is different. If we try to change without first accepting who we are, we risk creating more false images of ourselves. But if we accept ourselves for who we are at this very moment, we change because we want to grow and evolve with life; love is no longer the condition for change, it is the starting point for change. This is the true meaning of unconditional love.

CHAPTER 2

Understanding the Personal Dream and the Dream of the Planet

Our mind's main job is to *dream*—to perceive and project information onto a linear reality framed by matter when we are awake, and onto a nonlinear reality without a material frame when we are asleep or daydreaming. Our existence continually travels back and forth between these two types of dreams, or forms of perception.

The Personal Dream

First, there is your Personal Dream. No one else will ever know what it is like to live life through your point of view.

I might know you for years, but I will *never* know what it feels like to be you. I cannot know what it feels like to be in your body. I will never know, for example, what coffee tastes like when you drink it; I can only know this from my point of view. I am alone. I was born alone, and I will die alone. There is no one else living in this body, and there is no one seeing life through my eyes. Your beliefs, and your beliefs alone, belong to you. You are the only one who is with you for your entire life. Imagine if you didn't like yourself. That would be a tough life, because there is no escaping yourself. Regardless of how much you may distract yourself, you can never escape your own point of view.

We have many different kinds of relationships in this life, and they last for different durations of time. There are people who have been in my life forever, like my mom and dad. And there are others who I hope will be in my life for a long time, like my wife and my children. Other people might come and go more quickly—friends, coworkers, acquaintances. But no matter what the case may be, eventually we will have to say goodbye someday as the moment to move on arrives.

You perceive and project your life and your dream. This dream is constructed through your thoughts and your experiences of being alive. You experience your dream through the nervous system in your body, through your eyes and ears, through your emotions, through your love. You are the only one who knows how wonderful it is to feel that pleasure of eating a meal you enjoy, of hugging or kissing someone, of simply being alive, through your own perception. This is your Personal Dream. You can make it the most beautiful paradise or the most perfect nightmare; it is all based on what you believe in, what you think, what you know.

The Dream of the Planet

Every living creature is in communion. The communion between us can be as small as you and me or it can be as big as a household, a community, a nation, a continent, and so on. Along this line, the Dream of the Planet can be as small as a dream shared between just two individuals or it can be as large as a dream shared amongst everyone in existence—and anywhere in between.

What constructs the Dream of the Planet? It starts with you and me. Just as I am responsible for me to the tips of my fingers, you are responsible for you to the tips of your fingers. We are two individual dreams, two individual points of perception. This relationship between us, however small it may be, is the dream called *us*. It happens when we interact with one another and the ideas, concepts, and agreements flow between us.

The Dream of the Planet is composed of our yeses and nos—also known as *intention*. For every yes, something is created. For every no, there is no creation. With our imagination, we can create things that might be beautiful or ugly, and as soon as we say yes, the action is taken to manifest that thing. The Dream of the Planet is constructed by our collective choices; is the manifestation of our shared intention.

We are all connected because we have a desire to engage one another. We are now sharing a piece of a common dream, and this is the Dream of the Planet. You see, the Dream of the Planet is constructed by that need to share and communicate with one another. We either engage each other in a relationship based on respect, or we impose and subjugate each other disrespectfully with a need to make each other fit the mold of our own beliefs and ideals.

The person I am right now is the accumulation of my yeses and nos over the course of my life, and that is true for each and every one of us. Action is taken on a large scale when enough of us say yes. This is how the Dream of the Planet moves and acts. A good way to visualize this is to imagine a flock of birds. Amazingly, the birds are all flying in unison, but as soon as one lead bird changes the pattern, the other birds say yes and follow. Sometimes the flock splits in two, each group saying yes to a different direction. Sometimes they come back together. The birds who followed said yes to that direction. Now think about this flock as a community of people. Whoever controls yes controls the Dream of the Planet. Remember, the Dream of the Planet is as small as you and me, and it is as big as a nation—or the entire world.

On a smaller scale, when there are just two individuals, whoever controls the yes controls that relationship. This is why people often try to impose their beliefs on one another or, conversely, why they may subjugate their will to another's point of view. Harmony exists when we engage one another with respect, honoring each other's yeses and nos as we construct the dream of us.

Both the Personal Dream and the Dream of the Planet are built on knowledge. This is the tool by which we are able to survive in the world. But, as we will see in the next chapter, as our attachment to knowledge increases it narrows our ability to perceive life as it truly is, thus narrowing our potential.

CHAPTER 3

Knowledge and Attachments

If my attachment to what I know blinds me to all the available options, then my knowledge is controlling me; it is controlling my intention, and it is creating my Personal Dream for me. But with awareness of my attachments comes the opportunity to take back that control and to live as I choose.

Ever-Changing Meanings

> I am only responsible for what I say; I am not responsible for what you hear.
>
> —DON MIGUEL RUIZ

Symbols are representations that allow us to understand one another's experience of life. Words are symbols whose meanings and definitions give order to our experiences and allow us to communicate what we know. Words have an appealing but also very necessary and utilitarian function: they are the primary symbols allowing us to understand one another and create the agreements that build the Dream of Us, the Dream of the Planet. Take for example the word "sun." In all of its translations, it is a symbol that represents the entity that illuminates our solar system. In the Toltec tradition, the sun represents the creation of life, where the Earth is the mother, the sun is the father, and the merging of the two creates life.

A symbol's meaning is derived from agreement by a community, a culture, a nation, and so on. A definition is created by consensus—and when enough of us say yes to that representation, we call this *knowledge*.

For example, right now you are holding a book. "Book" is a symbol that represents the object in your hands. I could point to a book and you would know what it is because you can directly perceive it and you have past experience with it. You can still understand the concept of a book and visualize one even when neither one of us is holding one because of a previous tangible reference.

There is very little at stake in agreeing that a bound collection of paper with words on it is a book.

However, there are symbols for ideas and concepts that we all manage differently based on our own perceptions and points of view. Love, spirit, morality—these symbols represent concepts that are defined by an agreement but can never be fully understood by someone else's description or explanation. These symbols are virtual in the sense that they are intangible. When we use symbols to stand for concepts—whether we perceive them as good or bad or neutral—we are trying to give form to the formless. The more people who agree with us about a definition for an intangible concept, the more that idea seems to take form. This is why we refer to the Dream of the Planet as an illusion; the meaning of the symbols, the words, that construct our ideas and beliefs only feels solid through the agreement of the majority of individuals who are a part of that society or community. The building blocks of our society and our identity as a family or a nation are malleable and subject to change as individual dreams merge to create the Dream of the Planet through agreement and disagreement—yeses and nos.

For instance, when enough people come together and agree that a certain behavior is immoral—they have defined what it means to be immoral—that belief becomes more solid in appearance if a law is created reflecting that agreement. The people who engage in that behavior after the law is created are then labeled as "immoral" by the group that created the law. And if a law is broken, they will be punished accordingly.

But this consensus is an illusion because the idea of immorality never stops being virtual; it doesn't exist "out there" somewhere, it only exists in the mental agreements we make. In order to maintain the illusion, the symbol and the attached belief require continuous support by the group of people. That continuous support is the very fuel that increases an individual's attachment to a belief.

Because a virtual concept's solidity is dependent on the agreement, the need for it to be real can be overpowering and all consuming. The attachment to the belief in the form of a symbol can become so great that those who ascribe to it cannot conceive of there being any other belief that can take its place. These symbols feel solid not only because we might agree with these virtual agreements but also because we can take action based on them. When we take action based on our ideas, it seems like we have manifested them as reality. But a symbol's meaning is always still dependent on the agreement of an individual or society.

For example, there was a brief moment in time when a tulip was more valuable than gold. In the 1600s, during the Dutch Golden Age, the price of a tulip was ten times the annual income of a middle class merchant. The exotic flower, which was brought to Vienna from the Ottoman Empire in the 1500s, was in high demand for its beauty and soon became a symbol of status. When the mosaic virus decimated the population, making the wait for a single blooming tulip seven to twelve years (while also giving the infected tulips an even more exotic look), the price for the bulb skyrocketed. As a trader's market for tulip bulbs developed, people began selling their personal property in order to buy bulbs and resell them later at a higher price. Unfortunately for these latecomers, the infatuation with tulips soon fizzled and the market collapsed. When the agreement about tulips changed many lost their financial worth, resulting in a massive economic downturn. But the tulip never stopped being a tulip. The financial worth was the illusion. The nature of these types of agreements is that their definitions are always subject to change.

When looked at this way, we can see how fragile and transient our definitions and meanings of ideas and concepts are. We can also see the great power they hold. This is precisely why we invest so much of our energy in trying to prove that our definitions and our interpretations of things are right. This is the fabric that constructs our reality.

However, when we become so attached to that reality, and to the meanings of the symbol that constructed that reality, we do not allow room for change and growth. We may find ourselves struggling, fighting, arguing with others (and with ourselves) to maintain our beliefs and definitions of the way things work, becoming prisoners of our own beliefs. It is through those beliefs that we have constructed the story of us. No wonder they elicit such an emotional reaction. But by becoming aware of the nature of our beliefs, we have the power to change our stories and our agreements. Since knowledge is the bridge that allows us to understand one another, it is an instrument by which we can create the dream or the reality in which we want to live. Our intention, or will, is the force that gives knowledge its meaning, expressed throughout our bodies onto the Dream of the Planet.

When each of us expresses something, we express it from the point of view of what we know. Listen closely, but receive all words and other symbols with skepticism.

When you let go of your attachment to the meaning and the perceived truth that you apply to words and symbols—mine, yours, and others'—you have the freedom to step back and decide for yourself if those meanings reflect your experience in life. In addition, by openly listening to someone else's expression of their knowledge without holding an attachment of what those symbols mean, you have the opportunity to better understand them.

Attachments and Our Sense of Self

When my family and I were moving from Arizona to Northern California, my little girl Audrey was three years old and had been in preschool for about a month. She loved our Arizona home and her school, so when we told her we were moving and she would be starting a new school, she became upset. "No, Dad! My school! My house! Mine!" she cried.

In the days that followed, she clung to everything in her life—us, her toys, her best friend at school, even her school principal. My wife and I kept telling her that she was going to be fine. She would be in a new school with new friends and it would all be great. When we picked her up from school that last day, Audrey flatly refused to leave, hiding behind the principal's leg. In that moment, I paid very close attention to her. I imagined what the situation was like from her point of view: everything she knew would be going away. Her whole world was going to change, and she did not know who or what was going to remain. She grabbed hold of her friend Leo as he approached. "My Leo!" she cried. We eventually convinced her that it was time to go, and she reluctantly released her grasp on those things she had held so dear.

When we place ourselves in a safety zone where we feel comfortable and secure, and we are firmly entrenched in the this-is-who-I-am mindset, the worst thing imaginable is that it will all go away. And yet this happens again and again in varying degrees throughout our lives. When I believe something must stay in its rightful place, exactly as it is, for me to be OK, I have become attached to it, I have confused this external thing with who I am. If that external thing changes, and eventually everything does, how do I react? If I have placed my sense of self in it, then I have to defend it. I have to argue for it. I have to come up with definitions, and meaning. In short, I have created an attachment.

I know that I have put an attachment to a thing outside of myself when the fear of change takes hold of me. In change, the world I know can disappear, forcing me to go into the uncomfortable darkness of not knowing. But change is inevitable, and it arises time and time again throughout our lives: a relationship ends, we lose a job, leave a home, get a new wrinkle, a graying hair, or experience the death of a loved one, and so on.

If I look at all the things I have placed my sense of self in, I will find that my identity is placed in it. Fear comes when these things are threatened, because through my attachment I have interpreted these as being a part of myself; thus, an attachment is created to resist the possibility of that loss. When we look closely, we can notice how we're always defending the object of our attachment in one way or another. In essence, we are defending our definition of self. This is what my little girl does when she goes around claiming "Mine!" It's not just the object she is defending—it's her sense of self. I'm happy to report that as soon as Audrey walked through the door of our new house, she became excited. She ran into her new room and exclaimed, "My room!"

The challenge I have for you is to change your agreement, to see yourself as a perfect human being, and to realize that there is no object, idea, or knowledge that you need to be complete. You are perfect because you are alive in this present moment, transforming continuously with life. If we can see ourselves as perfect just the way we are because we are alive at this moment, we are free. Our attachments no longer define us. Instead, the knowledge we gather becomes a tool that can help us decide how we want to engage in dreams—the personal and collective—and how we choose to act is the manifestation of our intention.

Looking at the story of your life, do you take action as dictated by your attachment to knowledge, or do you use knowledge to take an action based on the awareness of your present moment? My grandmother asked me many years ago: Is knowledge controlling you, or are you controlling knowledge? You can answer this for yourself when you come to know how attached you are to your knowledge, your beliefs, or something outside yourself. When I was first confronted with this question, I did not know that knowledge could lead us astray, causing us to suffer unless we take the helm. I did not know how to answer my grandmother's question.

My grandmother believed that every attachment I form allows knowledge to control me. She spoke of heaven and hell, of demons and angels, of various levels of attachment and the consequences associated with them. This was her language, and it fit the experiences and context of her life. In the next chapter, I will explain the same teachings using an analogy reflecting our modern dream.

CHAPTER 4

The Five Levels
of Attachment

To start, I will describe the levels of attachment using a very simple analogy that allowed me to relate it to my life: soccer (or football, as it is known almost everywhere outside the United States). You don't actually have to like sports to get this analogy. In fact, you might even discover that not liking sports enhances your understanding of the concept. On the other hand, you might see an accurate reflection of your own level of attachment to a game or a team or recognize these examples in the people around you. Remember, you can apply the meaning behind this analogy to any situation you have in your life.

Level One: The Authentic Self

Imagine that you like soccer, and you can go to a game at any stadium in the world. It could be a magnificent stadium or a dirt-filled field. The players could be great or mediocre. You are not rooting for or against a side. It doesn't matter who is playing. As soon as you see a game, you sit, watch, and enjoy it for those ninety minutes. You simply enjoy watching the game for what it is. The players could even be kicking around a tin can, and you still enjoy the ups and downs of the sport! The moment the referee blows the whistle that ends the game—win or lose—you leave the game behind. You walk out of the stadium and continue on with your life.

At this level, you can enjoy a moment in time without any real attachment. You invested just enough of yourself to choose to attend or watch the game. This is you in total control of knowledge. You experienced the purest form of joy, stemming from your pure desire to experience life without conditions.

Level Two: Preference

This time, you attend a game—again, at any stadium in the world, with any teams playing—but now you root for one of the teams. You've realized that if you invest a little more of yourself by identifying a preference, the emotional roller coaster makes the game more exciting. You decide which team to root for based on just about anything—from the color of the uniforms to the names of the players. Perhaps you simply pick the home team. You spend the game rooting for one team but not necessarily against the other. Still, in the end, you walk out of the stadium and leave it all behind. At this level, you've invested a small piece of yourself in the game. You formed an attachment to something, however arbitrary, and based your decisions and actions on that attachment. You have engaged in a preference for a team.

You created a story of victory or defeat that shaped the experience, but the story had nothing to do with you personally, because the story was about the team. You engaged with the event and the people around you, but at the end of the game, you simply say, "That was fun," and let go of the attachment. This ability to attach and detach easily allows you to invest an emotional side of yourself that will enjoy the ups and downs of a great game. Life is happening, and you are able to share it with those around you, regardless of how they see themselves.

Level Three: Identity

This time, you are a committed fan of a particular team. Their colors strike an emotional chord inside of you. When the referee blows the whistle, the result of the game affects you on an emotional level. This is *your* favorite team. You can still go to any stadium or field in the world, but nothing compares to seeing this team play. Your team, winning or losing, partially defines your character beyond the ninety minutes of the game. You feel elated when your team wins; when your team loses, you feel disappointed. But still, your team's performance is not a condition of your own self-acceptance. And if your team loses, you're able to accept the defeat as you congratulate the other side. You accept the victories and disappointments as part of the emotional roller coaster that makes life interesting, but your self-worth is not based on these outcomes. If you meet a fan of the opposing team, you see not only a fan of soccer but also a fellow human being with whom you are willing to share a beer. You can sit together and discuss soccer and you can talk about how great you think your team is. You might even admit that you think their team is great as well. Your feelings and opinions surrounding your team are not a condition by which you relate to others or to yourself.

At this level, your attachment to your team begins to impact your personal life outside the stadium gates as you relate to the world as a fan. The separation isn't quite as clear as it was at first. At Level Three, this culture, this team, has become a small part of your identity. When the event or moment passes, it still forms who you think you are. You take the knowledge with you and begin to shape parts of your life around this team, bringing it to other environments that have nothing to do with it. For example, if your team loses, you might have a bad day at work, argue with someone about what or who is responsible for the team losing, or feel sad despite the good things going on around you. No matter what the effect is, you've let an attachment change your persona. Your attachment bleeds into a world that has nothing to do with it.

Level Four: Internalization

Staying with our sports analogy, at Level Four your association with your favorite team has now become an intrinsic part of your identity. The story of victory and defeat is now about *you*. Your team's performance affects your self-worth. When reading the stats, you admonish players for making *us* look bad. If the opponent team wins, you get angry that they beat *you*. You feel disconsolate when your team loses, and may even create excuses for the defeat. Of course you would never sit down with one of their fans in a pub for a friendly chat! You might even find yourself consumed with finding out more information about the players. On the other hand, each and every word of praise your team earns feels as though it is directed at you. Not only have you brought the game home, you have completely incorporated it into your persona, shaping your identity by your belief of what it means to be a "real" fan.

Although the team—the "piece of knowledge" in this story—has nothing to do with you in reality, your self-importance correlates with your attachment. Your life and your attachment are so blurred that everything starts to revolve around this team. Your fellow fans had better behave, too, because they all represent these colors, and these colors mean something: they have value in your life. They had better fit what it means to be a real fan. Otherwise, they shouldn't call themselves one. You find yourself debating how much better your team is outside the context of the game. You believe that anyone who doesn't agree with you is wrong. This is the point where the belief has moved from an identity to internalization. When dealing with the fans of opposing teams, you will argue and shout, but it will stop short of fisticuffs. You can still limit your defense to just arguing. While you may have some friends who are not soccer fans, you much prefer the company of those who think like you. As your attachment grows, you might make your loyalty to this team a condition by which you allow others to be in a relationship with you, including yourself. In other words, you have internalized your attachment to such an extent that it has become a condition of self-acceptance. Thus, you begin to impose this image onto the people you love as well as the people you interact with in your everyday life.

Level Five: Fanaticism

At this level, you worship your team! Your blood bleeds their colors! If you see an opposing team's fan, they are automatically your enemy, because this shield must be defended! This is your land, and others must be subjugated so that they, too, can see that your team is the *real* team; others are just frauds. What happens on the field says everything about you. Winning championships makes you a better person, and there is always a conspiracy theory that allows you to never accept a loss as legitimate. There is no longer a separation between you and your attachment of any kind. You are a committed to your team through and through, a fan 365 days a year. Your family is going to wear the jersey, and they better be fans of your team. If any of your kids become a fan of an opposing team, you will disinherit them. *Out!* At Level Five, your family can easily be torn apart and destroyed if any one of you turns your back on the team. Relationships mean nothing to you unless they are a believer in your team. Every action you take, every decision you make, is within the rules that you think make a great fan. Of course, you can't see anything from the point of view of someone who does not share your love of your team. If you did, you would be considered a traitor by your own standards. At Levels Three and Four you may still have friends who do not like soccer, but at Level Five you don't waste your time with people who don't love the sport. They do not know better. You choose not to have them in your life, and you are willing to fight for what you believe in. Your belief becomes more important than the experience. As your attachment grows, it can reach a culminating point where respect is lost even for humanity. In your eyes, a true fan is willing to die and kill for his team. It doesn't even matter if the referee blows the whistle to start or end the game. It doesn't even matter if they play soccer. The symbol and the colors are more important than your own life or anyone else's life.

Whenever we believe something without question, we are at risk for attachment at this most extreme level—and it can exist in the most unlikely places. If you are having difficulty relating to the sports analogy at this level of attachment, let me conclude with two real-life examples. At the end of one soccer season in Europe, a big name club was relegated into the second division, a lesser division. After witnessing that team's final loss, a fan went home and hung himself. For him, life was no longer worth living if his team wasn't in the Premier League. In another instance, a bus driver was a fan of a team that lost the Champions League final. He was so upset by this that he drove his bus into a group of people wearing the winning team's jersey. Four people died for wearing the "wrong" colors. This man's attachment to his team was so great he killed for it.

Fortunately, murder and suicide due to a favorite team's loss are rare occurrences. But when we turn to topics such as religion, politics, or our ideas about money, sex, and power, the examples of attachment at this level are numerous. Turn on any news station and it's easy to see. It's important to realize that when we, or anyone else, become attached to a set of beliefs at this level, it is easy not to see the humanity of an individual since we can only see the personalization of an idea that we stand against.

At Level One, you can go to any church, synagogue, temple, mosque, or drum circle, and you will find and feel the love and grace of God. At Level Five, God just happens to be the focus of devotion that the religion is centered on; in other words, the religion is more important than God. Imagine spirituality, homeopathic remedies, or veganism. Apply the levels to race or ethnicity or sexual orientation. Apply it to love. The Five Levels of Attachment can be applied to any form of information, and suddenly the consequences become far less trivial.

While soccer is a good introduction to the Five Levels of Attachment because it breaks down the concept into fairly understandable parts, the purpose is for you to see how the levels play out in your own life. As I explain the levels in detail in the ensuing chapters, you will begin to think about how attached you are to your various beliefs. You will learn how to assess what level you are on for every belief that you have—not as a basis for judgment, but to perceive a deeper understanding of self. The goal is to shift your perspective and see the potential that is present beyond your beliefs, and notice how your understanding of love and respect changes as your attachments' hold on you diminishes. Lastly, as we move through these next chapters, keep in mind my grandmother's question: "Is knowledge controlling you, or are you controlling knowledge?"

CHAPTER 5

Level One
The Authentic Self

"Is knowledge controlling you, or are you controlling knowledge?"
 I am a living being regardless of my knowledge, which exists only because I exist.

The first level of attachment represents the Authentic Self, the living being that is the full potential of life. It describes that force that not only animates the body but also gives life to our mind and our soul. The Authentic Self is always present, and it is only our attachments that keep us from remembering who we really are. From this place, our name is an empty symbol whose definition or meaning is determined by our agreement; the action of making that agreement is the first expression of "me."

When we were born, our parents lifted us up and held us in their arms. They envisioned endless possibilities for us in their love for us. They saw the unlimited potential of our Authentic Self—the life force that could take any action in any direction that would lead to those possibilities. But as we grew up, those possibilities diminished, as our vision of what we were able to do and be became narrowed by our attachments until we believed we had little choice in life. The truth is that we narrowed our possibilities by our own will. Yes, it is true that the Dream of the Planet can narrow our possibilities if we wish to play along with its rules; but the agreements we make with ourselves matter most when it comes to being able to manifest our intent. This is because a simple no in our own mind can stop us from taking any form of action. That is how powerful our agreements are.

We never stopped being the potential that our parents envisioned for us when we were babies. The only difference is that as adults we now have control of not just our body but also our mind. We require no knowledge to be our Authentic Self, and our awareness of this is what allows us to use knowledge as we engage the world, using our body through our mind as the vehicle that allows us to take action in life.

It is a beautiful symbiotic relationship of action/reaction through which we are able to experience a connection, a communion, between ourselves and all of creation. In all of our traditions, we hear the lessons of the wise men and women who teach us the beauty of life and how to let go of illusions, reminding us of our true essence. This is a moment of harmony with everything and the energy of life that courses through us. Every world religion and spiritual tradition has a name for the moment when we become aware that nothing but harmony exists. In the Toltec tradition we would call this *being in constant communion with our creator.* The only thing that separates us from one another is our point of perception; together we make a whole.

Engagement is the action of interacting with the focal point of our attention. As we engage life, we naturally go up and down the levels of our attachments, like a flower continuously opening and closing as days pass by. Sometimes we let go of our awareness as we increase our attachment to a focal point; other times we remember our authenticity as we let go of the attachment. But regardless of our degree of attachment, we are always our Authentic

Selves; we just simply forget that as we move up the levels of attachment.

With the practice of awareness we develop a discipline, a strengthening of our will that allows us to remain in a state of harmony longer . . . if we choose to. Many religious and spiritual traditions in the world have created a discipline that fosters this harmony, such as prayer, meditation, yoga, chanting, and dancing, among many others. This knowledge is an instrument of transformation, and experiencing it is the manifestation of the Authentic Self.

I used to think that the world's greatest masters of every tradition were the best examples of the Authentic Self. But now I realize that everyone I know and see is a personification of the Authentic Self. We are all creating, producing, learning, engaging, and loving life. We are all the personification of life; we are always the Authentic Self. We simply make the choice to see it in ourselves and others.

There is a moment when the Authentic Self becomes no longer an abstract term, but an experience. I believe we all experience such a moment. It could be during meditation, while painting or dancing, working or working out, lecturing or talking, making love, eating, or playing. It's the moment when judgment stops and pure harmony takes over.

For me, I have crossed that threshold from concept to experience while jogging—usually around the one-mile marker. This is when I am no longer thinking about my route, pace, or even the pain in my legs. This is a moment when everything goes calm, and all I can feel is my breath, the stride, and the environment. My mind suddenly shuts off and I am completely in the moment, and I know exactly what I am doing without the need for thought. From this place, even the term Authentic Self disappears, along with the rest of my thoughts. I am simply alive with the complete freedom to love myself and everybody as I choose. I have no need to distort the information I perceive because my perception of life is unencumbered by any attachments. The Authentic Self is the harmony of mind, body, and soul as the expression of Life. To tell the story of the Authentic Self is to tell the story of life, regardless of where humanity may be in the form of an individual's awareness.

When we reside at this level, we have the freedom to choose how we want to engage the Dream of the Planet. The awareness that we are the living being that gives life to our beliefs, to our knowledge, lets us choose with complete freedom where we want to place our intent and create, for as long as we choose to engage it by our agreement. Our will is set with the full awareness of our intent. Knowledge is alive in our minds precisely because we are alive, and that knowledge is the tool by which we can communicate with the rest of the world.

In this state of harmony we have the potential to love unconditionally because we have no conditions for self-acceptance, just a willingness to engage love with a respect for self and others. If someone were to say or do something insulting when we are residing in Level One, the Authentic Self, it wouldn't bother us. Their words and actions would fall off us like loose garments, as there is nothing in us for them to stick to. Because our love is not based on a behavior that we agree with or find acceptable, we love them even through such instances. From here, every possibility is available to us: We have the freedom to evolve as life evolves and to engage the people we love without the need to domesticate them to our point of view.

CHAPTER 6

Level Two
Preference

"Is knowledge controlling you, or are you controlling knowledge?"

I use knowledge as the tool by which I engage my preferences in life.

At the second level of attachment, we still move with the awareness of the Authentic Self. We recognize our ability to attach ourselves to something as we engage in the present moment, but we are also able to let go of the attachment when the moment has passed. We see ourselves as a reflection of life in the Dream of the Planet, and we attach and detach ourselves with ease simply by recognizing and letting go of that reflection.

Here's an example: Do you remember playing make-believe as a kid? I recall that before beginning the game, we'd all discuss the roles we'd be playing. Then, we would each draw from our knowledge of what was needed to create a mask that resembled us in that role so that we could play. Next, we would take on the persona of that role. Our faces would change as soon as we started playing, and our behavior would be adapted to fit the battlefield, the hair salon, the dinner table, the hospital, or even a day in the office. What made these games so much fun is that we used our imaginations and played our parts to create a fantasy world in which we could all engage each other in different scenarios, as if we were playing in a dream with others while we were awake. As much fun as it was to engage in these games with our friends and family, when the game was over, we took off the mask that was created by our knowledge and went back to being ourselves.

At Level Two, we have the awareness that knowledge is a tool that provides us with the information we need to make choices about where we wish to place our attention and take action. But at this level we don't distort the information we perceive, and we are using it to engage only in this moment. We can choose to adapt in accordance with the present life situation without losing the awareness of our Authentic Self, without the need to project a false image of self. In the Toltec tradition, this is called *controlled folly*—the awareness and honoring of self as we engage the people around us who project an image, or mask, onto us. Our awareness allows us to see the temptation to become attached to that projected mask, but we maintain clarity. At this level of attachment we don't forget we are playing a game, which makes it easier for us to detach once the game is over.

This awareness allows us to live without needing to distort knowledge to fit our individual points of view, our attachments, and thus, knowledge at this stage is still our ally. It is not corrupted by our sense of self-importance or any form of conditional love. Our relationship with knowledge allows us to engage life as it is; we are able to make choices with our reason as we perceive the difference between truth and distortion, and knowledge is a clean and perfect reflection of life.

From the Toltec standpoint, this is the *clean mirror*—we see every situation as it is, unclouded by smoke. We have the awareness that knowledge is the perfect reflection of life, and we are life. We have the awareness that the act of engaging in life is an act of love, and because we are choosing the direction in which we want to go and how we want to live, this is the act of unconditional love for ourselves. By approaching our lives as a work of art based on our own self-love, this allows us to unconditionally love the people in our lives for who they are without needing to domesticate them to see our point of view. Respect for the manifestation of our loved ones' own individual dreams, whether or not we agree with their choices, is always present at this level of attachment. Our love for self allows us to give love to the community. After all, we cannot give or share what we don't have.

Every thought and idea that forms our belief system has power only through our agreement in the form of yes or no; and it is our preference of how we want to engage the Dream of the Planet and life.

The word *Toltec* means "artist" in English, and life is the canvas for a Toltec's art. I am aware that knowledge is an instrument by which I am able to interact with the world, and my yeses and nos are the chisels or paintbrushes by which I create. I engage in the Toltec tradition by choice, fully aware that the name Toltec refers to an action or agreement belonging to a philosophy. Not calling myself a Toltec wouldn't lessen my agreement or the lessons I learn from this oral tradition. This means my agreement is not subjugated to an identity, my knowledge is not in the form of a mask that gives meaning to my definition of self. I am free to choose to agree, disagree, scrutinize, and engage with the Toltec philosophy, or any other, as much as I want. I am free to relate and engage in relationships with people who have a preference for another tradition or philosophy. I can change my mind when I no longer fully agree, or I may agree with it my whole life. That is true with every belief I have: I engage it for as long as I want to engage it, knowing full well that I am a living being with the full potential to experience life with or without that agreement. This is what gives power to my agreements; I make them because I want to. This is my art, my agreement: to allow myself to experience life in its ever-changing truth with love.

Think about an individual who chooses to eat healthfully, and through her search, she has chosen as her preference to follow a vegan diet—a diet that includes no animal products. She uses this knowledge to inform her choices when she eats, but she does not use the knowledge to identify herself as "vegan," nor does she use the knowledge to domesticate herself or others by it. If she chooses to have ice cream, she can do so without self-judgment and then reengage the vegan diet afterward if she so chooses. She uses knowledge to engage her preference with regard to her nutrition without ever losing her awareness of self.

Now substitute the example of a vegan diet with a lifestyle choice of your own. Do you engage in this choice with preference, or is it a rigid framework by which you judge your self-worth? If the latter, you know you are attached at a level beyond preference.

Our attention gives direction to the bridge that allows us to express and share with one another our knowledge of life—the agreements by which we construct our relationships, as well as express our preferences. With awareness, knowledge remains the bridge of communication between us, a clean foundation as we construct the Dream of Us. In our shared dream, it is my preference to be in this relationship at this moment and to love everyone, as well as myself, unconditionally.

CHAPTER 7

Level Three
Identity

"Is knowledge controlling you, or are you controlling knowledge?"

I identify myself with my knowledge, although I use it to see and understand the world.

We have a need to name, describe, and understand the things we engage with in life. Knowledge allows us to understand the world and the universe, but when it comes to understanding ourselves, our identity is a symbol that can be wrapped up in an expression of our knowledge.

From the stance of knowledge, identity is the grounding sense of self that allows us to have our place in the

Dream of the Planet; it gives us a point of reference by which we identify and engage with one another. But this identity is a mask that blurs our awareness of the Authentic Self, an attachment at this level occurs when we identify ourselves with our knowledge.

In the Toltec tradition, the mirror is still a clean reflection at the Identity level, but it is here that we begin to lose the awareness of the line that separates life and the reflection in the mirror. This is where we begin to believe that the reflection is the truth.

The main condition for acceptance in the Dream of the Planet is that our identity is recognized in a world of seven billion souls. Although we do not domesticate ourselves forming this identity (domestication occurs in Level Four, Internalization), by adopting it, we are hoping to be understood by our community, and thus ourselves. In wanting to be heard by the Dream of the Planet, our voice takes on an identity to express itself—or so we think.

When we use knowledge to construct the Dream of Us, or the Dream of the Planet, our identity is the mask by which the Dream of the Planet will understand us. When speaking mind to mind, knowledge recognizes knowledge, so we become attached to the mask of our identity. At this level we forget that the mask of our identity is an empty symbol—just like a word whose definition is subject to an agreement set by us and the use of knowledge in the Dream of the Planet. Just as language can change over time, so, too, can our identity mask.

As we increase our attachment to our identity, knowledge and consensus become very important to us, to the point where they give us meaning in life. So we construct the mask of our identity by becoming the embodiment of our acquired knowledge in the form of our passion. This is a mask based on our preferences in life.

Everyone we meet has a name and an identity with a meaning to go along with that name. Identity can be based on things like the color of our skin, the nationality of our family, the religion we practice, the political party that best reflects our beliefs, the sports team that allows us the excitement of winning and losing, the work we engage in every day, and the activities we love to participate in. Our name and identity give us a purpose and a sense of belonging.

For example, think of the people you know and the identities either they have assumed or you have ascribed to them: Patty the Teacher, Scott the Fireman, Joe the Next-Door Neighbor, José the Brother. What identities have you adopted for yourself? How do you portray those identities in the world? When you are at Level Three, you confuse these identities with who you really are.

As adults, we still have the ability to play make-believe like we did when we were children—that is, we still have the ability to create a mask based on our knowledge of how to engage one another in a particular setting. But as adults, the mask becomes a way to adapt socially and relate to a group with whom we are interacting, and we have forgotten that it's just a mask. . . . We think the mask *is* us!

To return to a sports metaphor, consider how non-football fans can get so involved in Super Bowl parties. Knowing that it's fun and exciting to invest something of oneself in the game, non-football fans will likely choose a side to root for, eagerly climbing aboard the emotional roller coaster of the game. But when the game is over, whether or not the favored team has won, a person at the level of Preference (Level Two) will be able to walk away from the game detached from the moment.

Now contrast that with the fans who may be out of sorts for days if their team loses, or incredibly jubilant if their team is victorious. Having forgotten to remove the mask, they are attached at Level Three. At the Identity level, the Authentic Self has the mask of the attachment in the form of identity.

This level of attachment can feel great when your team wins, or when things are going your way; but as life shows us, what goes up must come down, and no one wins all the time. That is why suffering inevitably occurs when you are attached at this level: we won't always be able to get what we want; but instead of having a preference and moving on if things don't go our way, at this level we have become attached.

Let's continue with the example of the vegan woman. At this level, she now calls herself a vegan, the symbol of her preference, even when she is not engaging in a meal. Her identity as a vegan gives her a purpose and a place in her community, and when she makes choices, her identity as a vegan is reflected. If she were to have ice cream, she may feel disappointed in her choice, but after a short time she will forgive herself and move on. She does not place unreasonable conditions on herself for self-acceptance based on her identity, nor do her friends and family need to be vegan in order to be in her life. She still has respect for others' manifestations of their Personal Dreams, just as she has respect for her own manifestation.

These are the hallmarks of Level Three: we have donned the mask of identity and forgotten it is a mask. This forgetting of who we really are, the Authentic Self, leads to some suffering, but generally not an inordinate amount.

In the next level, Internalization, our attachment to knowledge becomes more pronounced, domestication occurs, and we cause suffering for ourselves and those around us.

CHAPTER 8

Level Four
Internalization

"Is knowledge controlling you, or are you controlling knowledge?"

My identity, in the form of my knowledge, gives me the rules and guidelines by which I live my life.

The fourth level of attachment, Internalization, describes a degree of attachment to knowledge where our identity becomes the model by which we accept ourselves. This is domestication through attachment.

At this level, our narrators have begun to set the conditions by which we domesticate our identity. They measure our acceptance and rejection of ourselves and others based on the beliefs we use to construct the mask of our identity. We will distort the information we receive to reinforce the conditions of what we expect from life. The narrators also serve our need to validate who we are in our Personal Dream, as well as the face we present to the Dream of the Planet. Our knowledge is corrupted; it is no longer a clean reflection, but a Smokey Mirror.

Our sense of self is the personification of our beliefs, and our will is subjugated by the need to fit in with the Dream. Thus, our mask may not necessarily be in the form of our passion, but we will wear whatever mask we think we need to be accepted.

At this level of attachment, our focus is on internalizing an idealized version of our identity, and we may project a false image of self to secure our acceptance. This is the direct result of our domestication through conditional love. Acceptance is the reward of domestication, while rejection is the punishment. Although these conditions for acceptance and rejection may not be as rigid as the next level of attachment, they are learned and ingrained through the constant interaction we have with others. We use these conditions as guideposts for accepting and rejecting other people, but also (and especially) ourselves.

The attachment is to the mechanism of acceptance and rejection itself, which corrupts knowledge to fit our sense of self and influences how we relate with life. At this point, we've lost our respect for self and others, and conditional love is all we know.

One day, I had just gotten back from being in the park in Teotihuacán, Mexico, and decided to go to my hotel room to rest for a couple of hours. I turned the television on to a program in which two young women were combing a beach in Mexico looking for the "the best and worst fashions on the beach." They were both dressed stylishly, and as they walked the beach with confidence, they critiqued and ridiculed whomever they judged to be poorly dressed. The camera would then zoom in on unflattering shots of the unsuspecting beachgoers. In the segment, it seemed like everyone received a failing grade—the two hosts were apparently the only well-dressed people on the beach. Toward the end of the segment, however, they ran into someone they deemed to be even better dressed than they were. One of the hosts walked up to the fashionable lady, showered her with praise, and asked her to share her fashion wisdom. The change in the hosts' demeanor was incredible: they went from being unmerciful judges to subjugated followers.

As I watched the show, I couldn't help but think back to my teenage years, where walking down the hall was very much like this television show. I had been both the recipient of criticism and the critic myself, working on an image where adulation was the expression of acceptance. I remember feeling uncomfortable when I was the focus for not meeting the standards of one group, and I remember how righteous I felt being the critic in the group I identified with.

This kind of behavior isn't limited to appearances or trends—it occurs in spiritual circles, in the workplace, and in many other facets of life. The mechanism of our conditional love—the judge and the victim—has been mastered by many individuals.

I have seen some people turn the identity of a Toltec into a catalyst for their own domestication by turning the agreements for pursuit of personal freedom into conditions of acceptance, even rejecting others who engage in traditions that are different from ours. So it doesn't matter what the belief is, attachment at this level will corrupt it.

To continue with our dietary example, let's say the person who calls herself a vegan now uses her identity as the catalyst for her conditional love. In order to be worthy of her own love, she must be a strict vegan and not stray, lest she feel the wrath of her self-judgment. She surrounds herself with other vegans who will confirm the worthiness of being a vegan by accepting and judging themselves and others. She limits the people in her life who are not vegan and will try to domesticate the people she loves to change their diet, feeling pity for them for not being awake to her point of view. Thus, she is in constant conflict with points of view that do not side with her own. She is still eating a healthy diet, but she is imposing onto herself and others the knowledge that goes along with her preference in life; her mask of identity still reflects a passion of her Authentic Self, but the smoke has created a distorted image of that truth as domestication has set in.

Only unhappiness stems from the judge and victim mentality. To live up to these conditions and be accepted, we hide who we really are not only from others but also from ourselves. We are completely confused, believing that the mask we have created is who we are. We create what we believe is an acceptable image for conditional love, regardless of our passion and preference in life, and project that image solely for the purpose of acceptance. The image of a *luchador* (a Mexican professional wrestler) comes to mind, always fighting for fame and fortune. While he is keeping his enemies from taking his mask off and exposing his true identity, he is also trying to take off his opponent's mask so that his shines brighter with glory.

Attachment at this level results in disharmony between mind, body, and soul, and this is reflected in all of one's relationships. The only glimpses of peace come through individual victories, and these moments are far from permanent. This is the version of the Dream of the Planet that appears to be in constant conflict.

CHAPTER 9

Level Five
Fanaticism

"Is knowledge controlling you, or are you controlling knowledge?"
My knowledge controls my every action.

Level Five, Fanaticism, describes a rigid attachment to knowledge with an excessive intolerance of opposing views. It is driven by a need to believe in something one hundred percent, even though that something's meaning is dependent upon the agreement of others. Anything that contradicts or puts into question the sustainability of the belief is a direct threat, and a fanatic will defend the belief at any cost. Prejudice, intolerance, and violence are the instruments by which the belief is imposed onto the Dream of the Planet.

Regardless of how it can appear, the driving force behind fanaticism is not hate or anger, but rather an extreme form of conditional love for self and others. This is how any beautiful belief in the world can become lost in corruption, as knowledge controls a person's will for the sake of its own existence.

With fanaticism, a person's beliefs have fully and completely domesticated them, and knowledge becomes rigid and controlling. It has a tight grip on our will. Attachment at this degree requires us to try and domesticate everyone around us, and we become tyrants. There is no freedom in tyranny. In the Toltec tradition, the smoke does not let us see that there even is a mirror. The smoke is all we see.

For example, to illustrate this level on a small but far-reaching scale, I turn again to our young vegan woman who is now a mother. She domesticates her son to fall in line with the family tradition of being vegan, in an effort to give him the identity that she is convinced is the only correct one—the identity she has adopted for herself. (Please keep in mind that my objective here is not to judge veganism or make any of these examples a catalyst for debate; I only want to present a mirror.)

Imagine a dinner at this family's home. The young mother is making a meal in the kitchen while her husband and son sit at the dining room table.

"What would you like to eat?" asks the mother.

"Carne asada," replies the boy.

"We don't eat carne asada in this house," she says in a serious tone.

The boy begins to protest and pleads with his father to support him. The father, who has adopted the mother's belief system, responds by asking the son to listen to his mother. The child reiterates his plea for carne asada, as his mother responds that the rest of the family only likes healthy vegan meals.

"We are vegans," says the mother.

"No! I am not a vegan," says the boy.

"Okay, then you are going to have to find a new place to live," says the mother.

The mother's attachment to this ideal has led to a condition for the child: that to be a member of the family he must be a vegan too. This is domestication, as the reward for the child to eat a vegan meal is his acceptance as a member of the family. If he does not, he will be rejected by his family. Under Level Four, Internalization, there is still space for the boy to say no with the possibility that the mother will not follow through with her condition. But when the attachment becomes fanatical, the result is unrelenting conflict and domestication, and any contrary response leads to absolute rejection.

Imagine this situation in a family where the attachment is between a father and daughter about differing political beliefs, or a brother who is fanatical about the healing properties of homeopathic remedies and a sister who is fanatical about the healing properties of traditional medicine. This is an unrelenting war, where passion is replaced by obsession—an obsession to live up to the conditions of the mask of our identity—and whoever wins reinforces their attachment as the righteous beacon of knowledge that will awaken everybody to their truth.

This type of interaction within families is not uncommon and could also be applied to religious beliefs, social status, and so on. This is a case where one feels they must impose their beliefs upon other members of the family and will not cease until they are successful at subjugating the other's will or until a loss of the relationship occurs. This is the real consequence of fanaticism—a wedge between people who would really love one another if it weren't for this argument.

I have seen people become fanatical about the Toltec

tradition as well, where the concepts and lessons of personal freedom in the agreements and teachings aren't as important as the need to impose the philosophy on themselves and others as the only truth.

"I only want to be around people who are enlightened by the Toltec philosophy" is a comment I have heard on occasion. I have also heard criticism for not being "Toltec enough." It doesn't matter what the belief system is, if someone is fanatical, they have let their happiness and acceptance of others be dependent on adherence to that belief system. This form of unrelenting conflict can take a person to the point where an idea or belief is more important than their own life, let alone the lives of others.

Stories of honor killings throughout the world—regardless of religion or social status—embody an extreme form of conditional love within a family. From a point of view where a person's behavior is forced upon them under conditions of life and death, the Dream of the Planet can be seen as a nightmare: death in the name of love. When it is possible to be so attached to a way of life that the lives of our own family members are considered less important than upholding family values, then imagine what the extreme form of this level of attachment is capable of when it comes to perfect strangers.

The most obvious examples of fanaticism can be found in news reports that describe killings in the name of some cause, belief, or way of life—where one's love for their fellow man is entirely conditional upon the others' willingness to do or be exactly what is expected and acceptable within that belief system. The narrators speak so loudly in these cases that they drown out the Authentic Self completely and relentlessly impose conditional love to such an extreme that death is a means to the end.

Attachment at this level doesn't present itself only in the form of death, but where the violence of torture, rape, or any desecration of another being—be it man, woman, child, or animal—becomes a viable choice and action. Fanaticism is the complete loss of respect for another living being, when we no longer see an individual as a living being, and instead only an idea or a number. Unfortunately, there are many stories that illustrate this in the news and sensationalist media, but know that the individuals who take such actions all suffer from a form of illusion in which they believe they are justified in taking such actions.

Fanatics also impose unrealistic standards on themselves, trying to fit a mold at the risk of their own life. This is the case with anorexia or bulimia, where a person is so attached to achieving a certain ideal that they can no longer see the truth of who they are, even when they see themselves in the mirror. The image of oneself can become so distorted that one's own perception of one's humanity is lost. There is no awareness that a line has been crossed; only an illusion remains. Death comes without the awareness of having decided to take one's own life.

These extreme examples of fanaticism are probably not something you, the reader, are experiencing in your own life. But an attachment at this level has other manifestations that are not so easily recognized.

Loved ones can do their best to try to wake someone from this illusion, but as with anything, the individual must have an authentic desire to change their mind; but that doesn't mean the loved ones should stop trying. A will or desire to live is the catalyst for that change of mind. Once that desire is found and respect for one's humanity is regained, an individual can begin to move down the levels of attachment. At this point, the illusion can begin to fade. This is true for both the aggressor and the victim; we cannot give what we don't have. Letting go of this attachment starts by respecting our own life.

There is still a lot of work to be done to let go of the illusion—the corrupted version of knowledge that no longer reflects life, but what our attachment wants to see. As we find that grounding desire, we begin to see a sliver of truth that acts as a foundation for our transformation. Though we still work to let go of illusion, we have found a moment of clarity . . . a truth, in the form of life, was chosen. In regaining respect for our own humanity and the humanity of others, we begin to become aware of the strength of our own will.

CHAPTER 10

The Biggest Demon

My father has always pushed me to question my knowledge, challenge my attachments, and discover new ways of understanding. And so, during my training, he would often present me with puzzles. One day he asked, "Miguel, do you know what the biggest demon in the world is?"

I thought for a moment, then shook my head no.

"It's love," he replied, with a slight smile playing on his lips.

"How can *love* be the biggest demon in the world?" I responded doubtfully, feeling my emotional reaction coursing through my body, its epicenter somewhere around my belly. I felt the irritation of a child who knows his father is about to burst another one of his favorite bubbles.

"Solve the puzzle, and you will find out," he said.

I looked at my father, the man who had written the book *The Mastery of Love*, in disbelief. "Love can't be the biggest demon in the world!" I practically shouted. "We are all love. We all share love. Love is all we are."

To this, he simply replied, "Miguel, figure it out," and he walked away.

I thought about this, but it made absolutely no sense to me. We *are* love. We are born *into* love. How could he even say that love is a demon—and allegedly the *biggest* demon of all? And if I *am* love, how can *I* be the biggest demon in the world?

The puzzle sat unsolved in my mind for quite some time.

Then came my moment of clarity, the kind that arrives out of the blue and sets you on the path that guides you through the rest of your life. It arrived while I was watching the San Diego Chargers play against the Oakland Raiders, two football teams that share a big rivalry. I am well aware of my level of attachment to the Chargers. When I watch them play, I make a conscious choice to engage in the game, and I quickly go to a Level Three attachment. Sometimes I even go to a Level Four. This is probably why my epiphany came during a football game.

In the first quarter of this particular game, the television suddenly went silent. Something was wrong with the television or the transmission, and the game had *no* sound at all. I couldn't hear what was going on! Sensing an opportunity, I decided to assign myself an exercise. I challenged myself to watch the game as if I had never watched football before. My goal was to unlearn, or let go of, what I knew about football and simply enjoy the scene in front of me. I wanted to detach from all of my preconceptions.

It took me quite a while to stop describing to myself what was happening on the field and just watch the game unfold. I saw two teams in battle and began to understand their plays and actions from a fresh perspective. I began to see each action as if it were truth unfolding. My mind went silent, and I simply watched. A deeper connection formed between me and what was happening on the field at that moment. I was enthused by the play of both teams.

Somewhere around half time, the sound returned. And lo and behold, there were now two voices describing what was happening, narrating every moment. The narrators were telling me where to place my focus, and I could feel my attention being steered until I was no longer watching the game unfold as I had before, but instead was listening to what I was being told. The narrators informed me when to cheer and when not to cheer. They explained why the ball was thrown, why a touchdown was possible, and why the defense was doing so well. Then they started describing things that weren't even happening on the field: why a player held out on his contract, who should be traded, which player didn't deserve to even be on the team. I began to pay attention to only what the voices wanted me to see as they excitedly pointed out stunning plays and judgmentally expressed disapproval of weak players. When the game ended, I could only recall what those sportscasters wanted me to remember. Only glimpses of truth—a touchdown, a great tackle, or an amazing pass—shone through all that narration. Then the post-game show started, and every moment of the game was recounted. I apparently needed a team of narrators to tell me what I had just seen.

That's when I had my sudden realization: I have those same commentators in my own head. The only difference is that they have my own voice. Just like taking a sip of wine and thinking about the region and varietal of the grapes instead of enjoying the experience, I let the narrators talk about whatever catches my attention, and it is usually something I'm already attached to. This pulls me away from my experience of the present moment the way a rubber band stretched too far snaps backward. The narrators are the voices of the filter of what we know, the thoughts and beliefs that construct our belief system. This is what my father referred to as the voice of knowledge. I simply call them the narrators.

In the Toltec tradition, there is a symbol we use to describe all the chatter in our mind—the *mitote,* which means "a thousand voices all talking at the same time." Those voices are all trying to catch your attention, and the ones that speak the loudest are usually the ones that manifest in the form of an attachment. Some narrators may speak from distortion, while others may speak from truth. Through our reason we are able to tell the difference between the two, but it is difficult for us to tell them apart if we are attached to them. Depending on which narrators we are attracted to, we will perceive the world through their narration, thus creating our world in their image.

Of course I had always understood this on an intellectual level, but through this experience, I finally understood it on a much deeper, intuitive level. These narrators are the personification of our attachments to things, ideas, and beliefs. They can keep us rooted to past experiences as we try to make sense of the present. We have a predilection for fitting new experiences neatly into our preconceptions of life. These voices also keep us focused on some idealistic goal for ourselves, something to attain in the future, or something we might even convince ourselves we will never attain but think we should still strive for.

Turning our attention back to love, our narrators also play a major role in our relationships. In my own case, when I was younger I fell in love with a beautiful young lady. But after some time of just enjoying our love for each other, we grew comfortable and fell into a routine. At this point, we began to find some faults with the relationship and started to argue over what "should be" in order for our relationship to meet our expectations.

Other than what she told me, I had no idea what was really going on in her mind. However, I knew what was going on in mine. My narrators were commentating: "To be the perfect girlfriend, she *should* be like this . . . Our love is *supposed* to be this way . . . She does this to control me . . . How can I make her happy? . . . I *should* do this . . ." All the things my narrators told me were based on my attachment to what I believed a relationship should be in order for us to continue loving each other. All these expectations were informed by my past experience and the beliefs I had acquired growing up. I allowed my knowledge to analyze how a relationship is supposed to be, and I believed it. I was no longer connecting or having a communion with my beloved; my attention was on the voice of my narrators. At the time, I could see that while our love was still there, our attachment to the ideas about what we thought love should be would ultimately come between us. This was all a product of listening to our narrators.

And so, through this football game insight and the reflection of my relationship, I finally understood what my father meant when he said that love is the biggest demon. Instead of simply experiencing love, being love, narrators explain how love should feel: what makes us worthy of love; who should love us, and how they should express it; what we need to do or achieve to love ourselves, and what others need to do in order to receive our love in return. We begin to believe the narrators' analysis of what love should be and become attached to that belief; we begin to impose it on ourselves and others, thus creating a distorted reflection of love. Narrators convince us that if we can achieve an imagined perfection, we will be so full of love that life will be smooth going from then on. But what has really happened is we have made love conditional. And if we continue to follow the guidance of our narrators, we will go from childhood to young adulthood and beyond attached to the idea that we need to find a living personification of what "true love" is.

In order to be in love, we must have someone to love. And of course, that person is supposed to love us back. We get really hung up on this part—forming our idea of love through positive and negative reinforcement, much the way we do as children, always seeking our parents' approval, yearning for their acceptance and shrinking from their disapproval. This kind of love has so many conditions attached that suffering is inevitable. And, in this way, love becomes the biggest demon of all. Our distortions turn the angel of unconditional love into the demon, a symbol of the distortion of the truth, exaggerating our fears and distorting our view even more, creating a personal hell for ourselves.

When we look in the mirror and do not see a reflection of love, it means we can't see through the smoke that distorts our view and makes us think that love is something that needs to be gained, like the elusive carrot on a stick.

If we look at our reflection and into our eyes, we will see what lies beyond them, we will see the truth. There is no need to chase love, when we are love. We simply release our attachment to what we expect to see so that we can see beyond it. We turn off the volume on our narrators, the voice of our knowledge, and simply engage the present, and the true image of love will appear.

We have always been love. But we have grown so accustomed to the smoky, distorted reflection of love that doesn't allow us to see or accept ourselves that we don't know how to live life without it, which is the biggest lie. But when we become aware of our attachment and decide to let go of the distortion, then the motivation to change comes from our own love, and it gives us a whole new perspective on life. This genuine motivation is the subject of the next section.

When we let go of our attachment to our narrators—specifically their judgments and criticisms—and accept ourselves as we are, conditional love will no longer be the motivator that compels us to change. For example, if I look in the mirror and say, "Hey, Miguel, you are out of shape. No one will take you seriously if you look like that, you need to lose some weight," I am being motivated by the distorted opinions of my narrators. But when I look in the mirror and say, "Hey, Miguel, you are the perfect you in this moment, and I accept you completely, but I see that you might want to lose a few pounds in order to be more healthy," then I am being motivated to make changes by the desire to care for myself, which comes from self-love. Going on a diet is not a condition by which I accept myself. Rather, I recognize the truth of my unhealthy state, and I decide to make a change—not because conditional love has forced my hand, but because I love and accept myself.

Taking steps to improve our health, change careers, or really do anything that will transform our lives is often an emotional process. The fear of failure or of not obtaining the goal we set out to achieve often keeps us from taking action and actually perpetuates what we do *not* want.

In an episode of *Frasier,* a popular American TV show in the 1990s, Frasier is battling his past and has a hallucination of all of his former love interests. He comes to a conclusion that illustrates my point very well, saying: "I am alone because I am afraid to be alone!" He doesn't take a chance on love because he fears he will fail and then have to feel the discomfort of rejection. Fortunately, he realizes that the only way forward is to let go of the wounds that are holding him back.

Believing that we need to avoid rejection at all costs is a very common belief. For instance, if someone says to you, "I'm not attracted to you," you have a choice about what to do with that knowledge. You can accept the truth without the narrator and realize that it has nothing to do with you and has everything to do with that person and his or her particular taste. The news is still hard to hear, but it is simple, and it ends there.

Your other choice, and unfortunately this is a more common reaction, is to take that person's taste preference and use it against yourself to reinforce some negative belief you have: That person is not attracted to me because I am overweight, I am too short, etc. In this way, you end up using someone else's taste preference to convince yourself that you are not deserving of your own love or acceptance. The motivation to make improvements suddenly becomes conditional: If I lose a few pounds, maybe she will like me better or maybe someone even better will be attracted to me.

Either way, you are making a choice. You can choose to let your self-acceptance be subjugated by another person's taste or opinion, or you can choose to accept that they have simply stated what is true for them and that does not change who you are.

In my experience, the only motivator that brings lasting change is self-love. When I love and accept myself, I want to treat myself well and be as healthy as I can be, only then do I have the freedom to detoxify from whatever has been subjugating my will.

When it comes to being motivated by self-love to make changes in life, there are no musts or shoulds. The key phrase here is "I want to make this change for me." When you say yes to this choice, then you can begin the process. Doing it for yourself rather than to please others or to please your narrators makes all the difference between creating lasting change versus a temporary illusion.

Regardless of whether you stumble along the way, when you want to make a change, you keep getting up, exercising your will like a muscle in training. As your will strengthens, you will know what passion is. Passion is the expression of love, our Authentic Self, in the form of our intention. A goal—an end result—is simply a focal point that allows us to conduct our intention in that direction, enjoying the whole process that brings us to that point because we are living through it.

Authentic love is the greatest motivator for letting go of our attachments, while conditional love only strengthens our attachments. Knowing the difference is key as we enter the process of detaching from the conditions and agreements that keep us from experiencing our authenticity. At the root of this is how we relate to ourselves and the people in our lives: I cannot give what I don't have. If I have conditional love, I will give conditional love. If I have authentic love, then I will be able to give authentic love. The best way to let go of illusion is choosing to accept the truth as it is presented to us just as it is. As it has been said, "The truth will set you free."

CHAPTER II

Moving through
the Levels of Attachment

In my experience, the majority of people I encounter in life seem to be at Levels Three and Four—Identity and Internalization. Although the voices of fanaticism are certainly the loudest, those at Level Five seem to represent the minority of the people with whom I have interacted in the Dream of the Planet. However, it is important to notice that each of us moves up and down the levels of attachment during the trajectory of our life, and so we have all experienced different levels of attachment at one time or another.

We can move up and down the levels with awareness and sometimes without awareness, like a child who is hooked on an unpleasant moment until something else happens to divert or redirect their attention. Of course, as adults, our attachments are much stronger than this childlike experience, since we have a tendency to get very comfortable in our beliefs and circumstances. However, we can still change the focal point of our attention if we choose to go through the process of *redirection*.

Redirection

We must first become aware of where our attention is in the moment. Becoming aware of our attachments is the start of any process; recognizing which beliefs we have either become identified with, internalized, or fanaticized is the first step in moving towards our Authentic Self in any situation. Accepting the truth at that moment is accepting ourselves for who we are, attachments and all. From this point of acceptance, the question will be: "Do I want to keep the attachment?"

If we choose to keep it, and sometimes we will, that is fine, because we are doing so while being aware of the attachment and choosing to live life in that way. If we don't want to keep it, then we can make a choice to begin to let go. The freedom to choose between these two options is the manifestation of our intent, the power of choice.

As we grow more attached to what we believe, it is much more difficult to see the power of our intent. This is especially true when we have agreements that do not allow us to detach without first judging ourselves for even thinking of changing our mind.

Moving from Level Five to Level Four

In Levels Five and Four, Fanaticism and Internalization, the Dream of the Planet influences the way we view ourselves and how we behave. In other words, domestication reigns above all else. Moving from the extreme point of Fanaticism (the loss of humanity) to Internalization requires the ability to see that our life and all life is more valuable than any idea or belief.

Love and respect for self and others is the beginning to letting go of fanaticism. We cannot give what we do not have; respect for life starts with our own, and love is the grounding source for this respect. Seeing that our life is worth something allows us to see that the life of another individual is just as special. But to let go of the most extreme form of conditional love requires an ability to question the agreements that are tied to it. The act of questioning produces a moment of clarity that allows us to see our truth.

A consequence of this attachment to knowledge at the level of Fanaticism is that we impose self-judgment upon ourselves for even thinking that there may be another way in the form of questioning: For example, how dare I think of any other possibility other than Toltec? I'm a traitor to the philosophy! I should burn for this treachery!

When we are at Level Five, it is difficult to even question our attachments. However, questioning is indeed the way to break through the grip our attachment to knowledge has upon our will. This process is a bit like being on the monkey bars—the only way to move forward is to let go of the bar that is behind us as we propel ourselves forward to reach for the next bar. If we do not let go of the previous bar, we won't be able to move forward.

A moment of doubt in a belief can be the crack that will begin to expand our perception. Doubt in the form of skepticism with the willingness to learn allows us to withhold our agreement until we have clearly heard and considered everything that pertains to our belief. Skepticism makes it possible to reassess a belief and make a decision to hold on to it by saying yes or no.

Remember, there is a yes at the root of every belief we have, but a no can be enough to change our beliefs. Our no is just as powerful as our yes. This is the assertion of our will, and our becoming aware of it allows us the opportunity to no longer be subjugated by our knowledge. Here, we begin to realize that we—not our knowledge—are in control.

To recap, moving from Level Five, Fanaticism, to Level Four, Internalization, requires an awareness of the knowledge we perceive and then asking ourselves: Do I really believe this? Why do I believe this? Does this belief serve me? Reevaluating our beliefs introduces the option to continue to believe or to change. The mere act of exercising choice allows us to once again become aware of our own will. Letting go of Fanaticism is to allow ourselves to listen to what we perceive and reassess our willingness to say yes or no to it with awareness; to choose to redirect the focal point of our attention as we become more aware of the vast possibilities life is offering us. The best way to let go of illusion is to say yes to the truth when it is presented to us.

Moving from Level Four to Level Three

Moving from Level Four, Internalization, to Level Three, Identity, requires that we recognize our attachment to the mechanism of conditional love. Acceptance and rejection itself (our narrators' distorted commentary) is, according to Toltec tradition, the catalyst for the distortion or corruption of knowledge that allows us to internalize our identity. When we let go of that internal struggle between truth and lies, we cross over to Level Three, Identity. In our tradition, this rebellion represents the birth of a Toltec warrior: when we recognize that the mechanism has a hold of us, we make a choice to not believe in it, thus beginning an internal war for our own personal freedom.

My father's beautiful work, *The Four Agreements,* and *The Fifth Agreement*, a collaboration between my father and my brother don José, as well as the works of many other great spiritual and inspirational teachers and masters from other beautiful traditions, provide us with incredibly useful tools to help us move from Level Four, Internalization, to Level Three, Identity.

For example, when we make the choice to practice the Toltec agreements,

1. Be impeccable with your word

2. Don't take anything personally

3. Don't make assumptions

4. Always do your best

5. Be skeptical, but learn to listen

we begin to let go of those agreements and conditions by which we deem ourselves unworthy of our own love and begin to see our attachments from a perspective of objectivity. We also become aware that our attachment to domestication may even tempt us to use these Toltec agreements of personal freedom (or any such tools for transformation) as the conditions of self-acceptance and our acceptance of others. Thus, we distort these tools from the instruments of transformation that they are intended to be into the Five Conditions of our personal freedom.

How do we keep our choice to pursue our personal freedom from becoming the conditions of our own acceptance? We apply the lessons by our own choice and remain aware that they are merely the tools we use to guide our intent as we practice the mastery of our own self-love—in other words, we begin to use knowledge as an instrument to help guide our intent with awareness. This requires a choice to accept ourselves for who we are. The moment we realize that we can love ourselves just the way we are, we can see that domestication is no longer needed; our acceptance is no longer in the future. We are living that love at this moment. Becoming aware of our actions, taking responsibility for our own will, and repenting, if need be, allow us to forgive ourselves and others for our actions and theirs, which helps us to let go of domestication.

Exercise: Using a Labyrinth in the Toltec Tradition

In my family's Toltec tradition, we practice a method of forgiveness and letting go of our domestication, as well as our emotional wounds and poison, by using the labyrinth—a single-path maze. It is a symbol and ceremony used in various ways by many tribes and traditions of the world. The particular exercise that follows is performed in our Toltec tradition, but it is not the only way to use the labyrinth as a tool for transformation.

Envision yourself at the beginning of the labyrinth. First, you must be willing to enter. If you are not ready to forgive and let go, you have a choice to not enter the labyrinth. This exercise only has power if you say yes by your own will, and by your own will alone will you be able to engage in the exercise. If you do choose to enter, this is the action of saying, "Yes, I am ready to forgive and take responsibility for my own will."

As you enter the labyrinth, imagine it is a road map of your past that leads to your present moment in life. With every turn, envision a person, a moment, or a belief that you have used in some way to domesticate yourself. What or whom have you used to subjugate your own will in order to be accepted by yourself or others? When you hold that vision in your mind—a person for example—stop, envision him or her, and become aware of how their words have contributed to your domestication and say, "Forgive me. I have used your words to go against myself." Although that person might have used his or her words and actions to domesticate you, or to cause you harm or pain, you are the one who ultimately said yes to the belief and allowed it to blossom in your mind.

Becoming aware of your responsibility for your half of a relationship is crucial as well—it's not just the other person's fault. Recognize that you have been using someone else's words or past actions to potentially cause both of you harm, simply by saying yes. The action of saying yes is letting their words and actions impact you, allowing them to hurt you or go against you. Their words and actions have power to hurt you only by permission, because you chose to agree with them.

Forgiveness happens the moment you say no to carrying this pain, this weight, this hurt, and let go of it all. Say aloud or to yourself, "Forgive me, I have used your words and actions against myself, and I will no longer use them to hurt myself again." Forgiveness is the action that allows us to move forward in the labyrinth.

In my case, I can envision people who have judged me for the sake of domestication from their point of view: "Forgive me, I have used your words and actions against myself, and I will no longer use them this way." Of course I can also see the people who told me the truth, especially when I was hurting myself, and I thank them for their clear reflection of my actions.

Continue through the labyrinth, repeating the same action of forgiveness as new people and situations come to mind—whatever person or wound hooks your attention at that moment. That is the next one you are ready to face and to forgive. As you reach the end of a labyrinth, you may either find yourself at an exit or at a point in the very center. For the sake of this illustration, you will find yourself at the entrance to the center of the labyrinth. Stop here.

Look at the entrance to the center point and envision a mirror. Walk up to that mirror and see your own reflection. When you are ready, repeat these words: "Forgive me, I have used your words most of all to go against myself, and I will no longer use them to hurt myself again." The action of entering the center point of the labyrinth represents the moment you forgive yourself. This is the action of your own forgiveness and of reclaiming the power, or the impeccability, of your own word—of your own intent. You are worthy of your own forgiveness, as much as you are worthy of your own love.

At this point in this exercise, you have let go of the past by recognizing that the only thing that exists is this present moment. The labyrinth itself is now the past, and you can let it go as you forgive yourself. With awareness, you can now draw the knowledge from your past to make choices in the present moment. The labyrinth expands as you live your life, but the only truth is in that center, that present moment where you are alive. The labyrinth ceremony ends when you recognize that you are worthy of your own love because you are alive in this very moment.

This ceremony is a living symbol; it only has power through our intent. Like the active work of applying the lessons and writings of the masters and teachers who help us heal from our wounds, the labyrinth is meant to represent the active work of letting go of illusion. Letting go of our knowledge in the form of Level Four, Internalization, allows us to once again reclaim our personal freedom from the tyrant of our domestication as we move to the third level of attachment, Identity.

When we are no longer controlled by the distorted voices of our narrators, our identity gives our experiences significance and allows us to understand them by using our knowledge as an effective, helpful tool. Thus, our identity and our knowledge enable us to interact with the Dream of the Planet with a power we do not have when we are at the level of Internalization.

In order for us to relate to and be a part of the Dream of the Planet, knowledge needs to understand us. This is the function of knowledge: it fulfills a need to understand ourselves and the world in which we live. We use it to manage our experience of life and to express our impressions of it. The philosopher René Descartes' famous proclamation "I think, therefore I am" is the expression of this attachment to identity. But "I think, therefore I am" is uncorrupted by the mechanism of judge and victim since it no longer has to distort knowledge to fit the attachment; it simply describes what is without distortion.

The attachment to identity is the personification of knowledge as ourselves; we call ourselves a concept in an effort to make sense of our complex selves. The moment we let go of our attachment to identity is the moment we become aware of the separation of our being and what we know. Knowledge exists only because we are alive, and our will is the bridge between knowledge and ourselves in the form of our choice between yes and no.

Moving from Level Three to Level Two

Moving from Level Three, Identity, to Level Two, Preference, is the moment we become aware of ourselves without needing to identify ourselves. Level Three is like having a mask you don't realize you can remove. The moment you understand that the image of the mask is not you, you regain the awareness of your true self—an individual who is completely free to take any direction in life.

At the root of everything that gives form to our belief systems there is a yes. That yes gives life to an idea, a symbol, or a story because it has your intent. Each person's identity has a meaning because they give it a meaning by agreeing with it. Letting go of the attachment to an identity is recognizing that there is a clear separation between you (the Authentic Self) and knowledge. That line is your yes and your no; it is your intention.

When you recognize your truth, that you are a living being regardless of what you know, you are free to let go of the attachment of needing to know who you are, because you have the awareness that you are. When you authentically choose how you want to engage in your own life, as well as in the Dream of the Planet, the mask of your identity no longer has to shield your Authentic Self in order to have a voice. You are in control of your intention, your personal dream.

The hallmarks of this level of attachment are that you love yourself unconditionally in this present moment; you play in the Dream of the Planet knowing that your yes and no give life to your art; and you understand that truth exists regardless of whether or not you believe in it, while a belief only exists for as long as you believe in it.

Let's revisit the imagery of the Smokey Mirror through our Toltec Tradition. We've broken through the smoke enough to see the mirror as we let go of Fanaticism; we've cleared the smoke as we let go of Internalization; and we've become aware that the mirror only reflected the truth as we let go of Identity. Now, as we let go of Preference, we become aware of being the truth that the mirror reflects.

Moving from Level Two to Level One

Preference is based on an awareness of the Authentic Self, the living being that is me, and the willingness to engage life. We have the awareness that in the present moment can take any direction, but there is a preference for a certain direction. Regardless of that preference, or the action we may take based on it, the awareness of the Authentic Self will endure. We can engage completely in the moment or concept.

Moving from Preference to the Authentic Self is simply the act of disengaging from our preferences as the moment passes. We can then reengage (attach) or disengage (detach) at will when we choose to live in the moment.

What Is the Authentic Self?

> What's in a name? That which we call a rose
> By any other name would smell as sweet.

—WILLIAM SHAKESPEARE

The level of the Authentic Self is a name or term that simply describes the living being that has the capacity to engage life. Our Authentic Self is present throughout each and every level; we simply have filters that block our awareness of it. We can choose to be our Authentic Self as a being who is completely free from attachment, if that is what we choose to be. This state can be temporarily reached through meditation and other similar practices. (I say *temporarily* because our awareness normally fluctuates throughout our lives as we engage the Dream of the Planet and are tempted by the mechanism of the judge and the victim.)

The Authentic Self is the living being that gives life to our bodies, enabling us to perceive and project life and interact with the Dream of the Planet; it is the energy that moves this pen across the paper until the being leaves this body. It is pure, unlimited potential.

"What is 'me,' if it's not my identity or my Authentic Self?" is the question my knowledge asks of me. Even the label we are using—"the Authentic Self"—is a symbol to express something we want to understand. *Who am I?* This is one of the most important questions on the spiritual path. The answer cannot be put into words, yet I know that I exist. Just as I can say, "I am not this body," I can also say, "I am not this mind." I am just this living being giving both my body and my mind life—an empty definition whose meaning can only be determined by my yes or no.

The Five Levels of Attachment aren't rules or guidelines for "achieving" Level One, the Authentic Self. The Five Levels are simply a framework to help us become aware of where we are at this moment in relation to the various things in our life. We can look at any situation and determine what is driving our thoughts and behavior as far as a particular attachment is concerned.

With awareness of how attached we are to a particular belief or idea, we regain something very important: our ability to make a choice, to say yes or no all over again. The true freedom we have as individuals is to be able to choose with full awareness of what we want and don't want, instead of allowing our knowledge to dictate what we are supposed to be or choose. Our freedom to choose is true freedom; it is free will.

If we choose to remain attached to something that brings us pain, it is because that thing also comforts us in some way. Knowing this, we have the opportunity to further examine ourselves. If we are unaware, we go through life with blinders on, a slave to the distorted commentary of our narrators. But with awareness, we will be able to answer my grandmother's question: "Is knowledge controlling you, or are you controlling knowledge?" The answer is the truth of where I am at this moment, and the truth will set me free.

When you are ready to let go of an attachment, all that is required to begin is a willingness to say, "Yes, I want to let go." And that is the simple beauty of it. From a place of awareness, we no longer require the mechanism of the judge and victim to motivate ourselves. Our new motivator is passion, stoked only by unconditional love and recognition of our limitless potential to move forward in the trajectory of our choosing.

CHAPTER 12

Uncovering Our Stories and Assumptions

It's one thing to define and illustrate attachments in general, but it is quite another to recognize attachments in ourselves. This can be achieved by examining our beliefs and their effects on our Personal Dream. There is a difference between learning from our own experience in life and learning from what others tell us their experiences have been. Just like in the teachings of my family, I didn't understand until I was able to see a concept or trait in myself. It is my intention that the next section will help guide you on your personal journey of self-exploration.

Exercise: Uncovering Your Assumptions

Begin drawing a circle on a piece of paper until you are about three-quarters done, then stop. Even though you have not completed it, you can still recognize the shape as a circle. This is because the mind has the ability to make the assumption that we are looking at a circle and will complete it for us. The same is true if we draw two sides of a triangle. We see it as a triangle.

Based on our past experiences, our mind has the uncanny ability to fill in the missing parts when all the information is not available. This is the Gestalt principle of closure: our minds react to familiar patterns even though we have received incomplete information. Artists use this method when creating conceptual art, which is often quite thought-provoking and mind-boggling.

But the mind doesn't just do this with geometrical shapes. It fills in gaps to make assumptions about *everything*. The mind shows preference when adding information, too, and favors adding what it thinks it already knows—that is, it supplements incomplete new information with the beliefs it is already attached to. As an example, let's pretend I am a man who is brokenhearted over my last relationship in which my girlfriend left me for another guy. I have a new girlfriend whom I've been dating for a few months. I am waiting for her phone call. As time passes by I wonder, Why hasn't she called? It is seven p.m., and she should be finished with work. And then my mind attempts to answer my question. Here are some possibilities that my mind comes up with, based on my past experience, to "complete the triangle":

a. She is out with her girlfriends.

b. She is at the gym working out.

c. She is with another man.

Although I didn't have all the information, my mind came up with three possibilities. If I am unaware of my attachment to past experience that I label as knowledge, I will gravitate to the story that best fits my narrative: "She is with another man!"

Coming from a place of unawareness, my emotional reaction is to grab hold of this last assumption and think back to any time when she wasn't available for me. As I do so, my anger and my attachment grow, and my mind reinforces my insecurity with even more assumptions. Of course, that explains everything! I think.

At that moment the door opens, and in walks my girlfriend with shopping bags full of food and goodies. "Surprise!" she says. I turn around in anger, and shout, "You are cheating on me!" *BANG!* Fight.

Because I was still stuck on my last failed relationship, my insecurity was dominant, and the assumption that my new girlfriend had also cheated on me best fit my story-line. Coming from a healthier place, I could have attached myself to one of the other assumptions, or no assumption at all. But my attention went to the information that fed my insecurity because it felt most familiar to me at the time. This is the problem with making assumptions.

To make matters worse, we not only are predisposed to assume things, we also become attached to our assumptions and convince ourselves of their truth. They complete the missing line in the story so that we can grasp a "whole truth" by shining light (what we think we know based on our previous knowledge) into the darkness of the unknown. But it is a line of information that is not based in truth; it is a line that satisfies an internal need for resolution. We are willing to even distort this line so that life fits what we believe it should be based on prior experiences.

If the actions we take in life are based on information

we perceive, not having all the information can stop us in our tracks. Our sense of security is often dependent on knowing the big picture and taking the right actions, although we cannot possibly know everything. From that point of view, there is a need for assumptions to reinforce our sense of security. The more we are attached to a belief that offers us that sense of security, the more attached we are to the "correctness" of that assumption.

We are only one point of perception and cannot possibly be aware of everything. Therefore, one action experienced by many will have many stories to explain and justify it. Each person fills in their version of the story with the familiar lines of what they assume to be true based on their attachments. We are attached to creating a story about every action from our own point of view, describing, explaining, and fitting it into our own belief system. This is what we have been taught to do.

Let's say I stand up from where I am sitting, walk across the room, and kiss your hand. The kiss is truth. The missing information is: Why did I do that? What does the action represent? What does it all mean?

The answers to these questions are subjective and are based on what we already know and all the possibilities that are available within our belief system. Only I know for certain why I have kissed your hand. When we don't have all the information, often the first story we tell ourselves is closest to the truth. You may say, "Miguel kissed my hand to prove a point." But as we tell and retell our story about the event, we add on to the story, often coming up with less desirable possibilities, like in the example about my girlfriend not calling. Someone with distorted perception might end up convincing herself that I kissed her hand out of pity because she is getting old.

Believing an assumption is a choice, though if I am *unaware* that my mind is filling in gaps, then this is not really a choice at all. I am at the mercy of my assumptions. But when I have that awareness, an assumption allows me to consider a possibility that will only become true the moment, and *only* at that moment, when it comes to fruition. If the assumption is incorrect, with awareness I am able to simply release it, and new possibilities abound. Seeing our attachments for what they are allows us to see that an assumption is merely one possibility.

When we are aware that our assumptions are not necessarily truth but simply possibilities, little discipline is required to not act on them. We already know that an assumption is a story we have created that shows a possibility, and if life presents a different truth, then we detach from that possibility because it no longer serves us.

Exercise: Discovering the Foundation of Your Beliefs through Assumptions

Here is a little exercise for you: Tap into your memory and recall those experiences by which you made assumptions that were later shown to be untrue. Why did you make the assumptions you made? Identify the missing pieces of information and think about why you chose to fill in the gaps the way you did at the time. In almost every case, the stories you create will be based on your attachments to certain belief structures, and if you leave the source of these attachments uninvestigated, they will assuredly cause you future suffering.

For example, in the earlier fictitious example of my girlfriend surprising me with dinner, I had assumed she was late because she was cheating on me. If this assumption goes unchecked, the wound of her imagined betrayal would negatively impact my emotional sense of self and reinforce my faulty beliefs about relationships just as if it had been true. In other words, a wound that was created by an assumption will have a lasting impact as an attachment until the moment I see the fallacy of my assumption.

But you can't stop with just recognizing the assumption; the purpose of this exercise is to become aware of the foundation of your beliefs—especially the ones that have a negative impact on your life. When we build our belief structure on assumptions and we become attached to that structure, we are living in ignorance. The truth, however, is the path to freedom. Becoming aware of those assumptions, and the source of our attachment to them, allows us the opportunity to truly heal from a wound.

The Quest for Truth versus the Quest for Being Right

When you become aware of how attachment distorts and corrupts knowledge, you can begin to see how some people easily confuse the quest for truth with the quest for being right. These are not the same thing. The quest to be right is about self-importance: we need to be right in order to accept ourselves; this is a condition we place on our self-acceptance and our acceptance of others. The quest for truth, on the other hand, is the desire to discover—regardless of whether our beliefs are supported in the process.

Making a Choice to Accept or Reject Our Beliefs

My grandmother, Madre Sarita, was a faith healer. People who witnessed her actions would create fantastical stories about them, attributing magical qualities to her ability to help others achieve better health. They called themselves believers. Every time she healed someone, an observer would analyze and describe her actions, making it all sound so phenomenal and otherworldly. My grandmother would always say, "God healed this person, not me," yet others would still put their own spin on it and spread their belief to others.

Since these fantastic stories were about my grandmother, I really wanted to believe in them. I had witnessed many of the same events, as I saw many people truly recover from their ailments. But I began to notice that other people's perceptions of what had happened didn't necessarily fit mine. While I felt an experience, other people tried to explain it by calling it magic. Somewhere between the lines was the truth, but all the superlatives kept it hidden. This made it mystical and fueled fanaticism in those people who were firmly attached to such a belief. So at a young age, I had to learn to decipher what was truth and what was just a story. I learned to rely on my own perception but to question my own perception as well.

If I had tried to tell someone who insisted Madre Sarita had performed magic that they were misperceiving something about the action, they never would have believed me. After all, they were speaking of something they had personally witnessed and benefited from: *magic*. The believers would dismiss anyone who disagreed with them as not being able to understand. So I learned to let it go. As I became aware of my attachment to being right, my need to convince them to see it from my point of view was reflected back to me.

Later, I thought I could depend on things I learned in school to be true. After all, what I was learning was drawn from common sense and history. Then one day my father told me not to believe everything I was learning in school. In much the same way people had interpreted Madre Sarita's actions, people had interpreted the stories and ideas I was being taught. That news really threw me for a loop, but I came to understand that I had to look for the truth in *all* cases.

In Mexico, where I spent much of my childhood, there is a story that schools teach about six heroic cadets who defended themselves in the war against the United States. At the Battle of Chapultepec, the U.S. Army came into Mexico City from the west and tried to take over the palace. Six cadets remained, and they defended the palace and the city, but they fell one by one. Juan Escutia, the last of Los Niños Héroes, refused to be taken by the enemy. He wrapped himself in a Mexican flag and threw himself from the palace point.

When you go to Chapultepec Castle and see the area where he supposedly landed and then look to the stone marking the point from where he supposedly jumped, it seems impossible for him to have accomplished this feat. Modern historians refute this patriotic myth, and some say the cadets never existed at all, despite genealogical evidence. Fact or fiction, it is taught in history textbooks. Mexico is not the only country or culture whose textbooks contain stories rather than facts.

As a child, I believed the story of Los Niños Héroes because I didn't know better. Now, I have the choice to believe it or not. I know that within the words a feeling of patriotism can be found. That is truth, even if the story is false.

I choose to believe I am Toltec, a descendent of the Eagle Knights, because I choose to believe the words of my great-great-grandfather don Exiquio, who passed away when he was 116 years old. He was already an elder when my grandmother was born in 1910. His word stands. This belief is a leap of faith. My family may pass on the teachings of Eagle Knights, but are we truly descendants, as our oral traditions tell us? Knowing that our history is based on word in no way negates it. I also have to be honest in understanding that the stories we tell now contain generations of distortions and adaptations. Still, the lessons remain the same, and so I *choose* to believe in the lesson. That is my *preference*.

The stories that we tell about ourselves to make us feel comfortable and safe are simply history. We can choose to believe because we want to, keeping in mind that the stories do not describe the truth of who we really are. And we must be careful, as the very act of wanting to believe in these stories blinds us to the truth. Believing the stories without question or scrutiny ultimately leads to disillusionment, as we become attached to the identity we have created for ourselves through the telling of the story. Remember, a story can describe a moment, an experience, a lesson in life; but regardless of how clean a reflection of the truth it may be, it is still a story that we can choose to believe or not.

Things in our world go beyond reason and logic. But to believe—in the mystical, or in the scientific—without being skeptical is letting knowledge take control. The fantasy then becomes more real than life itself, to the point where we spend so much time looking for the spectacular that we don't realize joy can be found in the everyday occurrences happening all around us.

When we base our identity and self-importance on what we believe, regardless of whether it is in the earthly or the supernatural realm, we will find it difficult to be skeptical. And when we question everything we believe in, the foundation on which we have built our identity will prove to be shaky. But remember, self-confidence is being able and willing to question your own beliefs.

Many people believe that self-confidence means standing behind your beliefs one hundred percent. If you fail to listen to what else is going on in the world and only rely on what you think you know and believe, you've attached yourself to an idea that blinds. This is not confidence; it is stubbornness. We are conditioned to behave in such a way that whenever we encounter a truth that contradicts something we believe, we are quick to either reject it or create a story that protects our belief and further weaves a web of distortion. In so doing, we keep distorting our faith further, forming new beliefs to keep our sense of self safe.

The lesson here is to shift our confidence away from our beliefs and back to ourselves, since we are the living beings who give life to the beliefs in the first place. In other words, rather than having confidence in *what* we know, we have confidence in *who we are*. Instead of defending or debating a belief with all our might, we look and listen to what is going on around us. Questioning ourselves and being open to changing our minds about something does not mean that we must question our core being. With self-confidence, we can simply question our beliefs and the stories we've created to describe our being.

Ask yourself,

- Where did I learn that belief?

- How is that belief affecting me?

- Am I using that belief well?

- Do I still need that belief?

These questions can help you identify the things that inhibit your full potential. Consider a particular issue, action, or relationship. Are your past beliefs regarding that topic still true in the present? We often fear that changing our point of view is admitting that something about us is wrong. Thinking we have been wrong can lead to guilt, because actions we've taken and things we've said have been based on that one belief. If we decide that a belief is no longer working for us, it can potentially make us question every past action that was based on that belief. It does not have to be this way. Instead, we can choose to be aware that what works one day may not work the next. Things change, and we do not need to go back over each and every action. Our virtue has not been lost. Remember to proceed with self-love and self-acceptance at all times, as this is the only path to real and lasting change. In the next chapter, we will continue with the exploration of how being unaware of our attachments can cause suffering in our lives, especially when dealing with others.

CHAPTER 13

Recognizing the Role of Attachments in Conflict

Most of us have an ideal version of how we think the world should be. I *have to.* You *must.* They *should.* It *has to be.* When we hear these words, we are listening to the voices of our narrators expressing an agreement that is at a higher level of attachment. The narrators are reminding us how things are to progress within the framework of our understanding in order for the world to be the way we want or expect it to be. These are the rules we have created for ourselves to live by—and if we fail to follow these rules, we judge ourselves (and others) harshly. We have to get it "right," and our beliefs dictate to us what that means. Depending on our level of attachment to a particular belief, we may not waver in the least, remaining so closed-minded that we cannot even think about alternatives.

Whenever we hear someone say that the world should be such and such way, as beautiful as the idea may be, we must realize that it can be easily corrupted, because for the world to be in this ideal state, the idealist *must* impose his or her beliefs on others and subjugate those who refuse to fit in with their "perfect" image of the world.

Sometimes we think that the only way to make someone a better person, and, by extension, make the world a better place, is to convince them that they should see things our way. But there are plenty of people around us who don't behave the way we think they should, and we waste energy trying to convince them to be something they are not, instead of allowing them to be who they are.

When we think that we know more or better than someone else, we are setting ourselves up for a clash of beliefs. This is what corrupts a beautiful idea. The idea can be anything—organic food, civil rights, tolerance, animal rights, world peace . . . or any seemingly noble idea you can think of. A fanatical attachment to any of these ideas will create more harm than good. Once the attachment to the belief outweighs the importance of the message, it corrupts the idea; respect is lost, and freedom is compromised. Without respect for the freedom of choice, peace is not possible.

When we become so attached to these "noble" beliefs, we use guilt or place conditions on others to encourage them to conform to our standards. We know we are doing this when we hear ourselves say things like, "Aren't you ashamed of what you are doing?" or "How could you be so thoughtless?" To bend others to our will, we look for anything that tugs at their emotional structure—and when we cannot find any buttons to push, we may become even angrier and more uncompromising.

In the case of loved ones whom we feel are harming themselves through bad habits, we may think by instilling fear in them we can bring about lasting change: You must get help! You have to let me help you! You should not be doing this to yourself! Unfortunately, this type of approach simply causes more pain. Someone who is shamed into making changes isn't changing anything.

We are all free to choose our beliefs and create our attachments from our own point of view. There is no one master plan that we all must follow or perish! There are seven billion people living in our world, and so there are seven billion different points of view. If we each insisted that only our point of view is valid, then we would also have seven billion clashes in our world. As long as we engage in the I-am-right-and-you-are-wrong struggle, there will always be conflict. It is our attachment to being right—our attachment to our personal importance—that keeps us from experiencing freedom in both our Personal Dream and the Dream of the Planet.

Freedom of choice is not about being right or wrong; it is about opening up the channels of communication and respecting one another as human beings in order to create a community that we share with one another. When we become too attached to an ideal, the first thing that we lose is respect; first for the people around us, and eventually for ourselves. While our points of view may differ, we are all a product of the same source. The only thing that separates us is our attachment to our own point of view and our attachment to the belief that others must share it. This is where we begin putting conditions on our love for one another, and this is the source of conflict.

Defending Our Ideals

Once you are aware of your beliefs, you will be able to question your ideals and viewpoints. With awareness, this questioning will no longer shake your foundation. You will no longer find yourself defending your viewpoints or imposing them upon others.

If two people who have very different beliefs argue, the argument might never end. In an attempt to convince each other to change, to fit their version of what they each believe is true, they create a veil between them. Their inability to listen results in a lack of respect.

Although it may appear that one side is ahead for a while and then the other, as long as each side is attached to their beliefs, the battle never ends. It is only when one person is able to step back and listen to the other without judging that there is potential for a shift to occur. By consistently questioning our own beliefs, we open up infinite possibilities and avoid getting trapped inside a closed mind that only wants to be right.

We do not need to defend ourselves or our beliefs against other people's opinions and beliefs. Our only need is self-respect. When we have self-respect, we do not take what other people say and do personally. If we give in to the temptation to make someone else's actions a personal affront, we have lost that self-respect by saying yes to their agreement. Once we do this, the attachment to this belief makes it necessary for us to switch our motive from one of defense to offense. With one shift, we can easily go from being victim to aggressor, which has a whole new set of consequences. By not taking things personally we do not give in to our personal importance and can therefore make decisions based on mutual respect that will solve problems instead of making them worse.

Recently, a worker came to my home to install something. As I do with anyone who comes to my home, I sat and spoke with him, asking questions and watching him work. He asked me what I did, and I explained a little about what I do. He grew agitated, saying there is only one truth, only one way, and everyone else just wants your money.

He spoke about his pastor and the teachings of his church, reiterating that there is only one way. I didn't argue with him, I just listened to what he was saying. By my grandmother's application, that is learning. As he was leaving, he said to me, "When I die, I only have to answer to one person. If I'm wrong, well, I'll find out then."

He went on to tell me that the reason he believes is not because he had love or faith, but because he wants to get into heaven. That was his main purpose. At least that is what he said to me. He said, "Miguel, you can say whatever you want to all those people, but remember there is only one way, one truth."

Through listening to him, I had indeed learned something. He shared his belief system, but that is not what I learned. What I learned is that he honestly believed what he was telling me. And who am I to say otherwise? Had I felt the need to retort, this would have been based on my own attachment to my identity and my beliefs, and a battle of personal importance would have begun between us.

This worker showed me that if I had chosen to argue with him, I would be forming my own attachment to knowledge, which had nothing to do with him. This gave me the freedom of choice. I was able to look at my belief square in the face and chose to listen to both him and myself. How he chooses to live his life has no bearing on how I live mine. Although I can see how his attachments and his knowledge control him, I know that it is not my place to object.

Instead of blindly and deafly arguing a point fueled by our personal importance, we can at least be willing to admit that we might be wrong or that the situation can be looked at from an entirely different perspective, as in the case of the worker. When we choose to share our truth with others from this place, we can begin building mutual respect. When we look at our beliefs and viewpoints with an open mind, it becomes clear to us how attached we are to our own beliefs.

Being aware of our attachments allows us to regain power over our freedom to choose whether or not we want to continue to hold them. The choice is crucial. Sometimes we choose to root for our home team or debate religion or politics with our family. Sometimes we choose to devote a portion of our life to a cause or a movement, and sometimes we choose not to. Having awareness, however, will let us know if our personal importance begins to corrupt the essence of whatever activity we have chosen to engage in. If we find ourselves vehemently defending our position or cause, it means our attachment has crowded out our awareness.

Listening to what others say without giving their words power over us allows us to become aware of our own truth. It enables us to see what is real for us and what is just an illusion—a lie fueled by personal importance. The gift of listening will expose any illusions of personal importance. If we are coming from a place of awareness, our truth does not need to be defended through the ego-feeding mechanics of an argument. It requires very little energy on our part to simply state our truth, if we choose to state it. When the truth is simple, you know your foundation is solid. Of course, there may come a time to stand up for that truth. If that time comes, you can be confident that you are standing on firm ground with the full awareness of the power of your own will.

There comes a point in life when we grow tired of needing to be right—especially when we see how this ego-feeding need affects our relationships with people who just want to be our friends, with the beautiful souls who just wanted to love us. Our attachments don't let us see further than the tips of our own noses.

We all have a catalyst, a call to action, which moves us into making a change in our life. This catalyst almost always comes from outside of us, but as we become aware of how our filter of knowledge is constructed, we realize that lasting change only comes from within. Our changes affect how we interact with the people in our life and impact the communal dream—the Dream of the Planet.

I am the one who said yes and no, I am the one who made all of my agreements, and I am the only one who is able to change them. When I see how my attachments are affecting my relationship with myself and the Dream of the Planet, I realize that I am the only one who can change it. This is the awakening of our intention in the form of our free will.

As you embark upon the final chapter of this book, I wish to leave you with the idea that it truly is possible to engage in our human existence while seeing beyond our attachments and fully experiencing life. My intention is that the final chapter will provide you with the tools to help you exercise your free will. That is the power you have, and I celebrate that to the fullest. I only share my words; I have no power over you. As the words reach you, you are the one who says, yes, I agree, or no, I don't agree. That is the freedom of choice.

CHAPTER 14

Honoring Our Emotions

When we talk about it on paper, detaching or reducing our level of attachment to something doesn't sound so difficult, does it? If we find ourselves in an unhealthy situation, we walk away. If we fail to reach a goal, we try again. If we want to make a change, we move forward with our transformation. There is no need to complicate anything; we keep it simple, moving from one interaction to another without becoming too attached to any one outcome.

But in life it rarely happens this way. This is because we are human, not heartless robots. Our emotions rise to the surface, and we initially feel pain when we try to reduce our dependence on things outside ourselves—the things to which we are most strongly attached. So the question is, how do we deal with the emotions that arise on the path?

It's important to keep in mind that our emotions are real and should not be ignored as if they don't exist or stuffed away as if they aren't valid. Emotions create the most authentic anchor we have to ourselves. The whole spectrum of emotions—fear, love, jealousy, insecurity, anger, joy—is very real. But here's the thing: What triggers those emotions may *not* be real. At this point, you probably understand how this can be true.

Emotions help us communicate with each other. Without the ability to express what we are feeling and to recognize how others feel, we would be at some disadvantage. Take the example of my son, Alejandro, who is diagnosed with high-functioning autism. We are teaching him how to express his emotions so that we know what he is feeling and he can interpret what others are feeling. One of the tools we use is a teddy bear, a gift from his aunt, which shows different emotions. We are also teaching him the words that go along with each emotion. This is the most basic use of knowledge, and it is necessary for each of us to learn this throughout our lives, as early as possible, so that we can express our sense of self and convey our needs and desires within the Dream of the Planet. Some of us, like my little girl Audrey, are really good at sharing what we are experiencing emotionally. Some of us are not as good at it yet, like Alejandro. Still, an emotion is present with or without a label, with or without a facial expression. An emotion is truth.

Again, what we are experiencing is real, but what triggered the feeling could be based on an illusion or a distortion. Here is an example. I am holding my newborn son, Alejandro, in my arms, and I am filled with bliss. I am not thinking, I am simply allowing that moment to engulf me. The emotion is real; the moment is real. I have not created a story in my mind. Then, let's say that as I'm holding him, a little thought grows in my head: What if I lose him? All of a sudden that illusion, that insecurity, that fear, has stirred in me. This little seed of fear takes hold, and as I am exposed completely to the emotion, I feel that fear of losing my son engulf me. I go from a moment of complete bliss to a moment of pure terror. The trigger was an illusion, but I still felt the emotions.

Our emotions—regardless of the triggers—are expression of ourselves. These are the important questions to ask: Are we aware of the triggers? Do we know if the trigger is based on reality or if it is based on faulty information? Is the trigger based on an attachment to a certain belief or expectation?

Whenever I'm upset, I know that something I hold to

be true has been put to the test. I look at that agreement inside and out and ask myself, is it an agreement based on truth or illusion? If I am very attached to that agreement, I might end up using a lot of my energy to keep it alive. If I have to struggle that hard to give something life, it cannot be very solid, can it? If I become skeptical, I am giving myself a choice to once again believe that agreement or not.

Uncomfortable emotions are like car alarms: they let us know there is a problem to attend to, a wound for us to work on, thus allowing us to see our own truth. Whenever an emotion gets triggered, it is the opportune moment to ask questions such as: What is this about? What agreement is at the heart of this? What attachment does this threaten? Do I really believe this? Is it important? Answering these questions gives us the opportunity to examine our beliefs and choose whether or not to continue to believe.

We honor our emotions by realizing that they are an expression of how we feel and what we are going through. We look at what has triggered our emotions, while still allowing ourselves to simply feel. We further honor our emotions by having the awareness that they may have been triggered by something not based on truth. Thus, we use our emotions as a tool for transformation, because they completely expose whatever agreement has been hiding beneath the surface. I am grateful to my emotions for telling me my truth, for it is only through exposure that we regain the power to choose between "I will continue to agree" and "I am ready to let go."

Clearing Away the Smoke from My Reflection

When I look into the mirror, I perceive myself this way:

I am . . .

- Miguel

- a Toltec

- a nagual

- a Mexican-American

- an American

- a mestizo

- a husband

- a father

- a writer

and so on . . .

When viewed through the rules of my attachments, this is the list of self-definitions I might use as conditional models for self-acceptance. Where there are conditions for self-love, it is because my perception is controlled by internalization or fanaticism. However, without attachments, each and every one of these labels is just a definition that I can choose to either say yes or no to as part of my identity. I can simply choose one of these identifications as the preference by which I want to engage life for the moment.

My awareness gives me the opportunity to see my reflection as I am at this moment. The mirror is reflecting my truth: a physical body that is an empty symbol, much like the words in the above list, whose definition of self is dependent upon my agreements. Even without definitions, it is still reflecting a living being with the full potential to go in any direction. Regardless of the name we give it—even a name such as Authentic Self—it is simply reflecting life. Looking into a clean mirror, without the filters of my belief system (the Smokey Mirror), I perceive life as the "I am."

The clean mirror is the awareness that reflects the full potential of life. How I define myself and what I say yes or no to (the execution of my intention) are my choice. If I choose, I can call this awareness the Authentic Self—the representation of life in the form of this body. Whatever I choose, I see myself just as I am.

Imagine looking into the mirror and seeing yourself just the way you are at this very moment, without self-judgment. Maybe you become aware that there is something about you that is interfering with your health—physical or emotional. That is the truth of your body right now. When you are looking into a clear mirror, you do not make a self-judgment based on that truth, nor do you need to identify yourself as being unhealthy in some way. You simply look at yourself as who you are at this very moment.

Now, from a place of self-love, you can choose to take an action based on your perception, which, in this case, is seeing the truth of the condition of your health. This action is not a condition you place upon yourself to earn self-love; you love yourself for who you are at this moment. Whether you make a change or not has no bearing on this love. This isn't complacency; you are actively making a choice, and that choice is the action of your intent, your full potential.

There are 360 degrees of possibilities surrounding you. This point—this now—is your potential. To move forward in any direction is to make a choice; you say yes to something and no to all else. This is true regardless of whether or not you are aware of the infinite possibilities present in each moment. As described throughout these pages, the more attached you are to something, the more your vision is obscured and narrowed, sometimes to the point where you are convinced that there is only one way to proceed. Your attachment to a belief cuts off your ability to see beyond that one possibility. So, as you make choices to let go of attachments that no longer work for you, your options seem to grow and expand. But what you are really doing is increasing your perspective, as all possibilities are there all along.

Reclaiming Our Power and Gaining Our Freedom

As I mentioned in the introduction, my grandmother was my first teacher in the ways of our tradition, and it was through my apprenticeship with her that I learned to quiet my mind and trust my heart, allowing inspiration to flow through me. My grandmother also taught me the power of faith, especially in God, whom she credited for her abilities as a faith healer. In her later years she began waking up at three a.m. to pray and meditate with her rosary and candle.

Then she would begin healing, working, and consulting with people in need throughout the day.

When I completed college, my father became the teacher of our traditions. Through his guidance, I faced all the attachments I had created throughout my life, letting go to the point where my every wound was painfully exposed. In this way, I was able to heal from the pain of my own creation.

It is not easy letting go, especially when the things we believe about ourselves (even those that cause us pain) provide a familiar comfort zone. When we place our personal importance on knowledge and that is taken away, the crash is very harsh. Eventually, through the continued and authentic process of releasing our attachments, we find that who we are requires no justification to accept ourselves. This realization is very powerful; it's like letting go of the railing when you are certain you are free from any danger by falling.

At the time, my dad was spending time in Oceanside, California, and my grandma was there for a visit. Always looking for teaching opportunities, my father recognized an opportunity for a lesson.

"Miguel," he said to me. "Your grandmother is afraid of death. Help her to let go."

I looked at my father with astonishment.

My grandma turned to me and raised her eyebrows as if to say "Oh really?"

I swallowed. I did not want to do this.

"Miguel, help your grandma. Tell her why it's OK to let go of her fear."

I immediately got up, and as my grandmother had taught me so many years earlier, I cleared my mind, allowing myself to act and speak without attachment to my thoughts. My job was to help her let go of her final attachment: Level One, the Authentic Self.

I guided her wheelchair up to the big mirror in the hallway.

"Grandma, look at yourself in the mirror. You are beautiful. You are wonderful. You are the most passionate, smartest, and toughest person I have ever known. Imagine everything you hold to be truth—your family, your children, your Bible, your rosary, your incense, your candles. You have faith in all these things, and this same faith allows you to perform miracles for others. You may have said that it was God who healed people, and while that is still truth, it is also truth that your faith allowed you to do it. Your faith is so strong that everything you believe in comes alive with every breath you take. It is your attachment to this physical form, to which you give life, that keeps you from wanting to let go.

"Look into this mirror, Grandma, and imagine these things all around you that you hold dear. Your faith is so strong that you put Sarita in each and every single one of them. In the same way you have given life to your thoughts, your beliefs, and your ideals, these things are alive because of you. It is time to take your energy back from these things and release your attachments to them. Let go of the fear of what you are without them and what they are without you. When you take back your power from these things, you will no longer identify yourself by them. Then, there will only be you . . . you and your image of Sarita, your body. When you are ready to let go of this final attachment, you will pass away in peace."

Madre Sarita kissed me then and nodded. She passed away about a month and a half later. She lived to be ninety-eight years old, and she was always helping others. My love and gratitude for her are always going to be with me.

While we may not be talking about literal death here as we discuss the prospect of letting go of our attachments, we are talking about the potential death of how we identify ourselves—the things we love, the knowledge we have, the ideas we create. Everything we hold so dear is alive within us because of the energy we give it through our attachments.

It is easier for us to attribute a power to something outside ourselves than it is for us to see that *we are* the power that gives things in our world life. We are the ones responsible for ourselves and our reality. We are the creators of our own dream. This is why our self-judgment is so strong and alive with a force that can hold us back and rooted to the past—we gave our narrators the power! Fortunately, we do not have to die to reclaim it. Independent of the attachments that weigh us down, each one of us has the freedom to live life to the fullest at any given moment. The field of possibilities awaits our next step, and we can take that step confident in our ability to do so. When we are aware and see the truth of infinite potential, that is ultimate freedom.

Afterword

I have experienced a lot of life since I first started to apprentice in my family's traditions. I have felt the ups and downs of life—from confrontations to harmony, from feeling anger and fear to happiness and love. I have learned that the key to all forms of transformation is awareness. The starting point for any form of transformation is set on our willingness to accept our truth at that moment of awareness, a moment that moves with us along our path of transformation.

I developed an attachment to an outcome when I first started my work, but I continued into a process that goes beyond that attachment. I saw that there is an attachment to everything I have ever perceived—and only because I was afraid of the unknown. We feel most at ease with our safety net, of course, but as I began to move outside of that safety zone, the levels of attachment began to take shape and my understanding of my grandmother's lesson was reflected in my life.

We all want to be a part of a group or a community, to find that place that allows us to feel as one. We are always looking for that communion, so in the end, all of this work is about the ability to have a harmonious relationship with my brothers, my sisters, and myself. At first I thought it was about a quest to discover the hidden secrets of life, glazed with incredible stories of the metaphysical. But this practice really is about life itself. It has always been about creating a clear channel of communication with the people I love, starting with myself.

Understanding the Five Levels of Attachment is the beginning of reestablishing an unconditional relationship with ourselves. I start by recognizing that my life is worth something and that my body and my mind are the tools by which I am able to express myself—in love, intellect, and awareness. Knowledge turns to wisdom when the information that describes the world is a clear reflection of truth that flows and evolves along with us as we move through life. Love starts with me.

We don't all live in a monastery or an ashram where we are surrounded by people who are working toward the same end, allowing one another to enter into silence and work on our process. Rather, we live in the Dream of the Planet, where we are continuously interacting with people who find themselves at various levels of their own attachments. As we interact with others and want harmony in those relationships, the harmony starts with us. We become aware of ourselves and accept ourselves, and we are then able to give to others what we hope to receive in return.

The discipline of staying in that awareness while being able to relate to others is called "Controlled Folly." This mastery cannot be started without first becoming aware of our own truth, and the Five Levels of Attachment are an instrument that allow us to see our present truth with more clarity. As we begin to reconstruct our Personal Dream with greater awareness into our personal great work of art (which is always in progress), we have the ability to choose to create the most perfect harmony, if that is our desire.

In the end, it is all about seeing knowledge as the building blocks to co-create a dream with another person while maintaining our awareness of self. I enjoy interacting with the Dream of the Planet. I enjoy using knowledge to communicate my dream with you. I enjoy playing with the world that surrounds me with respect and love. I am a part of this creation. We can all become aware that it is love that bonds us to one another. We can love each other with conditions or with respect. The difference is harmony—a form of heaven on earth. When we have respect for one another's free will, then we have peace.

For me, home is no longer a physical place; home is me. It is everywhere my heart and love go. Wherever I am, that is where I call home. What better way to express our freedom than to let go of the wounds that have kept us oppressed? What better way to use my words than to say I forgive you? What better way to say I am free than to say that I love another without fear?

Let us enjoy this moment in life. The past is done, the future is coming, and the best way to say hello is by learning to say goodbye. I am love and peace starts with me. I do not see race, creed, religion, gender, or whatever else as a division of the human species. I do not see a belief that tears me away from my brother and sister. I do not see an ego, a personal importance that forbids me from communing with everything in existence.

The point of life is to love, and to do so is a choice. In that choice I take action, and in that action, I am love. I have a voice. I can use it to oppress, or I can use it to liberate. I can create, I can lead, and I can love. The same is true for you. Together we can say, I love.

All we have and are is love.

Acknowledgments

With all of my love, I honor my teachers: my grand-mother, Madre Sarita, and my father, don Miguel Ruiz.

My gratitude to my family for teaching me how to love unconditionally: my lovely Susan, my son Alejandro, my daughter Audrey, my Mama Coco, and my brothers don Jose Luis and Leonardo Carlos. My abuelita Leonarda, my abuelito don Luis, my aunt Martha, my Mama Gaya, my brother Ramakrishna (Trey), and my sisters Kimberly-Jeanne, Jennifer, and Jules Jenkins.

I want to express my immense gratitude to Randy Davila for believing in this project by being my publisher; to Carol Killman Rosenberg, for helping me find my center by being my editor; to Kristie Macris, for helping me find my voice to start this long journey; to Marilee Scott, for helping me find the ground to stand on; and to Janet

Mills, for your guidance and the continuous push for the essence of the word.

I want to pay tribute to all of my schoolteachers who taught me how to use knowledge, especially Jean-Pierre Gorin, for teaching me how to tell a story; Catalina Heredia, for believing in me and teaching me how to learn analytically; and my Theory of Knowledge teacher, Maria Esther Rodriguez Ruvalcaba, for reminding me that I really don't know anything.

All of my love and respect to my father's students who were also my spiritual teachers: Gary van Warmerdam, Barbara Emrys, Allan Hardman, Ted and Peggy Raess, Gini Gentry, Rita Rivera, and HeatherAsh Amara—you've all taught me so much love. And to the community that sprang from all of these teachings, my gratitude and love to you always.

About the Author

 At the age of fourteen, don Miguel Ruiz Jr. apprenticed to his father don Miguel and his grandmother Madre Sarita. From that early age, he was called upon to translate Madre Sarita's prayers, lectures, and workshops from Spanish into English. In this way, through constant repetition and review, he learned the content of her teachings in both languages. Through interpreting for Madre Sarita, don Miguel Jr. came to understand the power of faith. He saw firsthand how his grandmother manifested her intent to heal people, both physically and spiritually.

Don Miguel Jr.'s apprenticeship lasted ten years. When he reached his mid-twenties, his father intensified his training. At the apex of this power journey, don Miguel said to his eldest son, "Find your way out. Go home and master death by becoming alive."

For the past six years, don Miguel Jr. has applied the lessons learned from his father and grandmother to define and enjoy his own personal freedom while achieving peace with all of creation. Being able to apply his teachings to the world around him gave Miguel Jr. a new understanding of the lessons his father and grandmother had passed on to him, once again giving him the desire to pass on his tradition. After decades of training, Miguel Jr. was finally ready to share everything he had learned. As a nagual in the Toltec tradition, he now helps others discover optimal physical and spiritual health, so that they may achieve their own personal freedom.

Don Miguel Jr. is married and has two young children.

www.miguelruizjr.com

Hierophant Publishing
8301 Broadway, Suite 219
San Antonio, TX 78209
888-800-4240

www.hierophantpublishing.com